More
Stories
to
Hear
Again

by
Godfrey Nicholson

British Library Cataloguing in Publication Data.
A catalogue record for this book is available
from the British Library.

ISBN 978 086071 692 1

Commissioned Publication of

MOORLEYS
Print & Publishing
tel: 0115 932 0643 web: www.moorleys.co.uk

Introduction

A few years ago I was persuaded, most reluctantly, to publish a selection of Bible stories retold from the perspective of characters in the story. Most of them had been prepared for the Ladies' Meeting at the church where I was minister. Six years on and five years into ministry at a different church the stories are still being told. Various churches have invited me to keep telling them stories, and so more have been written. People like stories. That is why TV screens so many soap operas. Even when the story lines seem remote from normal experience, the characters draw us in to identify with their dilemmas and struggles, their joys and sorrows.

Jesus was a Master story-teller. His parables are memorable, even for people who know little else in the Bible. And as a Person the impact he had – and still has – on people is impressive. Trying to tell the story as it happened to people who met Jesus has refreshed the stories for me. It has underlined for me that these events involved real people, and that the change Jesus made was a lasting change. I hope that others who hear the stories again will sense that too, and know the powerful encounter with the living Jesus.

I have also worked with some of the parables. I don't for a moment imagine that I can improve on the originals, but perhaps I may achieve the more modest ambition of removing the veneer of familiarity which prevents us from listening to them.

Details have often been brought in from other Biblical material. Some details come solely from my imagination, and I ask your indulgence over these.

I am grateful for the encouragement that so many receptive listeners have given to me. I am humbled by how far the previous book travelled. I was startled to read it reviewed, and described as 'Narrative sermons / talks at their best!'

Suitably encouraged, a few of the stories have been used in the sermon slot in services.

At the end of the book I have included the Bible references where the original story can be found, together with some of the other passages incorporated in the retelling.

Godfrey Nicholson
2014

Contents

CHAPTER 1
While Shepherds Watched....

Christmas is coming too quickly, so I guess you will be getting ready for it? Written your cards? Got the tree and the decorations? Ordered the turkey? Have you started baking your mince-pies? The list of things to do seems to get longer every year. The only thing that grows faster is how much the kids want spending on them!

Will you be having a family gathering, as usual? It's funny, isn't it, how we all have our family traditions. We make a big effort to all get together at Christmas, and our family is no different. Mind you, it wasn't always that way.

One part of our tradition seems to start late on Christmas Eve, long after it has gone dark. We will be poking the embers of the fire, and Granddad will go misty-eyed as he stares at it in silence. Eventually he will start up: "Did I ever tell you ...?" It's the same every year, and we all chorus, "Yes, you did, Granddad!" He carries on just the same, as if he hadn't heard us; but you can tell by the twinkle in his eye that he knows just what is going on. He is going to tell us his story, his favourite story, and of course it is all about Christmas.

You can tell by looking at him that he spent most of his working life out of doors. He misses that life, of course, but he is too old for it now. His skin is weather-beaten and his face browned by so many years in the sun. They must often have sat around their camp-fires during those long nights, telling each other their stories. After all those years together, they must have known everybody's story just about word-perfect. We certainly knew this one, and in our minds we could picture every detail. Although we would tease him about it, actually we loved to hear him tell his story about that very special, that quite extraordinary night.

"It had been a long shift. We had been out in the fields all day, keeping a careful watch over the flock. They are very special sheep, you know. They are bred specially for the sacrifices in the Temple, so they must be free from blemishes and free from

1

injuries. Unless they are perfect in every way the priest won't accept them. We may complain that they are so fussy, but we still take a pride in what we do. If it is to be offered up to God, it must be the very best.

As the sun sank over the western hills, we settled the sheep down for the night, and began to settle ourselves down too. It was enjoyable, peaceful, sitting under the stars round the fire. At last we had the leisure to eat our sandwiches and have a refreshing drink. On a cold night a thermos would be welcome, but for much of the year a skin of new wine was good enough.

You still had to keep an eye on the flocks. Wild animals could come under cover of darkness and snatch an animal, especially a lamb. Occasionally one of the animals might take it into her head to go for a walk, and would need bringing back. It meant that one or two of us were able to snatch a bit of sleep, but there always needed to be some of us awake and alert.

We might pass the time telling stories, remembering special times. Other times it was the football results, and whether the manager should be sacked. From time to time there was a little resentment came to the surface. We grumbled about the Romans and their taxes; about this new-fangled census which would probably mean *more* taxes, and all these visitors who had come to register. We had a moan about the priests as well. They were keen enough to have the finest sheep and lambs from the flock. They expected us to keep close watch over them, night and day. And if we were doing that we could not get to the Temple to offer *our* sacrifices, and we could not get to the synagogue to share in the worship and the prayers. So, while we were keeping them stocked with their sacrificial lambs, they were criticizing us for not keeping their laws.

It seemed a night like any other, cool and starlit. The moon crept up into the sky, and after we had finished our meal and decided whose turn it would be to keep watch, we began telling our stories. Some were amusing, and some poignant. Some rambled on for ages; but when you've got all night, it doesn't really matter. Some were about what had happened to one or other of us or our families, while some were retelling what happened to our ancestors long ago. It felt as if by continuing to tell the story we were making it our own. Although it was our ancestors God had helped and saved, it felt as if he had done it for us as well.

Quite suddenly there was a dazzling light. It came so suddenly it terrified us, I have to admit. In an instant the whole field was as bright as day, and we had to shade our eyes. As we peered through our fingers to where the light seemed to be coming from I could see – an angel! Never seen one before (or since, for that matter). There he was, not many yards from me, as large as life, a shining angel.

"Don't be afraid," he said. My first thought was that it was a bit late to be saying that. If only he had given us a bit of warning that he was coming we might have been ready for him. You know, a bit of red carpet, a bit of something from the Takeaway, and a nice bottle to toast his health.

"No, seriously: do not be afraid. I have come to you with some amazing good news – capital G and capital N – real Good News!" When an angel addresses you like that you don't want to interrupt or to argue; so we waited to hear what this Good News was going to be. "It's Good News for you, and it will be Good News for everybody who ever will live. This will bring you more joy than you know what to do with!"

He went on, "Today, in David's town" (and he pointed over the way to Bethlehem), "Yes, over there, a Saviour has been born for you. He is Christ, the Lord." He paused a few moments for it to sink in. Maybe he was a novice angel, never been sent with an important message before. Then he added, "This will be the sign for you. You will find this baby wrapped in swaddling-cloths and lying in a manger." How very odd! I would not put my baby in a place like that.

We exchanged glances. This was really happening; it wasn't just a dream. Even as we were doing this, a great choir of angels burst into song, behind the one who had spoken to us. They were singing God's praises, for all they were worth, bursting with joy. I've never heard anything like it. And we had the finest seats in the house! It was almost as if they had been desperate to sing praises, and had not been allowed to. Now they had the chance they took it with all their might. It was a torrent of song.

3

"Glory to God in the highest, and on earth peace to those with whom he is pleased!" What a song they were singing! What a great God! If peace could remove our fears, then there was hope for peace on earth. From highest heaven, right down to earth: all of creation was part of the song. All of creation might share in the blessing.

After my initial shock, it was actually a disappointment when it had finished. The hills fell silent and the fields faded back into darkness, at least, until our eyes had adjusted to only having the stars for light once again. At first we could say nothing. Then we all started to talk. One thing we were certain about was that we hadn't imagined any of it. The angel was real, and we had really heard those amazing words and listened to them as they sang.

The real question was what he meant that a Saviour had been born. Was this baby the Messiah we have been awaiting for centuries? If so, then that was Good News for us; but hadn't he said it was Good News for absolutely everybody? For a start, I'm sure the Romans wouldn't think it was Good News to be sent packing by Messiah. Was there another way to save? That might save everybody?

"What are we waiting for?" I asked the other shepherds. "Let's go over to Bethlehem and see for ourselves." It never crossed our minds to worry about the sheep we ought to have been watching. It felt oddly as if they would be perfectly safe while we were on an errand like this – and they were.

When we got to Bethlehem a few minutes later we listened for the sound of a baby. There it was. Definitely and unmistakeably a new-born baby. The sound was coming from the back of the Inn. Hadn't the angel said something about a manger? And wasn't the manger round the back? Was this the place? We tiptoed to the door: I don't know why, since they would all be awake. We went in; and there they were. Mary was looking oh! so happy, but shattered. Joseph was looking proud and bewildered, just like I felt when my first was born. And there was the baby, wrapped in swaddling cloths and lying in the manger. The angel had got it right in every detail.

4

Of course they were surprised to see us. So we told them about everything the angels had told us. I saw them flash a look, as if each of them had been expecting something like this. I swear they almost said, "I told you so." Perhaps if this was such a special baby, they had known in advance. For all her obvious tiredness, Mary was paying the closest attention to all we said, and seemed to be trying to hold on to every word we said. "A Saviour, who is Christ the Lord." It had all seemed so strange to us.

Joseph told us how an angel had come to him – another one! – and told him that the baby had to be called 'Jesus' (which means 'God saves') because he was the one who was to save God's people from their sins. He would grow up to be the Saviour of the world. All of God's people, all those who would love him and trust him – he would save them from their sins. Then there would be peace on earth.

We stood and watched. Then Mary offered to let us give the baby a little cuddle, and he rewarded us with a smile. That old blessing came to mind: The Lord bless you and keep you (just like a shepherd would, I often thought); the Lord make his face to shine upon you and be gracious to you; the Lord lift up his countenance upon you, and give you peace. But now, the blessing of peace we prayed for the baby, with peace on earth to those who please God – that peace was to flow from this baby, and to us.

As I held him Mary told how an angel had visited her as well. Those angels had been busy! The angel had told how Jesus, her baby, was to be the Son of God, and how eventually he would reign for ever. No wonder all those angels had shown up! And no wonder they wanted to sing their praises! And to think that I was cradling in my rough shepherd's arms the very Son of God, the Saviour of the world.

Eventually, and very reluctantly, we agreed that we ought to leave them in peace, and to get back to our flocks. Were we excited! I wanted to sing, just like the angels had. I know, I know! I can't sing, but I wanted to! I had set eyes on God's Saviour, and the angels had told me about it. And now, all these years on, he has saved me and I want everybody to know him too."

Although I know Granddad's story almost as well as he does, I never get tired of hearing it. If that baby is the Saviour of the world, then it is worth hearing that story over and over again. Joy to the world, joy to you and me, and his peace to you now and always.

CHAPTER 2
A Wise Man Remembers

Saddle-sore? Too right, I am. And if you can get sea-sick in the desert, I feel that way too. Swaying this way and that for hours, days and weeks is definitely not designed for comfort. And that sun – I understand how it can drive you crazy.

But, was it worth it? Was it worth the time, the travel, the discomfort; and coming home feeling sick and sore? Was it worth risking looking terribly stupid? Absolutely it was! Would you like me to tell you more?

It all began a few months ago. One beautiful clear night we noticed a star that none of us had seen before. What could it mean, we asked each other? Well, from where it was in the sky, and judging by how brightly it shone, we soon agreed that it meant a very special king of the Jews had been born. Oh, I know we aren't Jewish, and their land is far to the west; but we remember some of them, and we remember some of the stories they used to tell. They told how their God had rescued them, and how he had promised one day to give them a great king. This star seemed so special that we felt it had to be him, and we must go and pay him homage.

We prepared gifts – you can't visit a new king and not take gifts to present to him, can you? But what should you take? Gold, obviously; after all, he is a king. And you can never go wrong with gold. What else? As we thought about it we remembered that the Jewish kings were also men who should live close to God, who ought to be men of prayer. Perhaps frankincense would be appropriate, as a symbol of prayer being offered up. The third gift was the hardest of all, and may seem strange: myrrh. Yes, I know; it's usually associated with burial, and we wanted to celebrate a birth and a new life. Yet some instinct that we all agreed on compelled us to think that a time would come when his death would be at least as significant as his birth – just don't ask me to explain why! So we prepared our gifts, and prepared ourselves for a long trek across the desert.

We said farewell to our wives and families, stocked up with provisions, and set off westwards across the desert. Reassuringly, the star shone brightly at night ahead of us as the camels plodded over the sandy tracks. Sometimes we stopped overnight with other travellers at taverns, or oases and palm trees in the desert. None of the other travellers knew anything about this new-born king, and were not that curious about him either. Some days we didn't see another soul, but kept on going.

We were certain that when we arrived in Israel we must go straight to Jerusalem, their capital city – but, amazingly, we were seriously mistaken. We expected that the whole city would be abuzz with news of a new king. We expected them to be excited and celebrating with parties and feasting; yet the first people we asked knew nothing. They directed us to the palace, the obvious place to go. The guards at the gate were suspicious, cautious, as we explained our business. They told us to come in, and promptly locked the gates to make sure we didn't hurry off. We waited a while, before one of the officials came. He told us to follow him, to meet the king. There he was, sitting on his splendid throne and surrounded by his servants. Some were fanning him, to keep him cool, while others were ready with fruit and wine.

"Congratulations, your Majesty," I said, bowing as low as I could manage. "Why?" he replied coldly. It looked as if he hadn't a clue what I was referring to, which was curious. Surrounded as I was by his armed soldiers, it was quite intimidating. Still, there was no getting out of it now. We had to explain everything we had seen and everything we knew. "We have seen a royal star in the east, telling us of the birth of a king of the Jews. We have come to pay him homage."

"A king, eh?" He looked puzzled. He thought for a moment or two, and as he did so he flushed with colour, and rage swept across his face. Even his servants looked fearful about what he might do or say next. "Call the priests, now!" he demanded. As soon as they arrived he shouted at them, "This king, this Messiah, where is he meant to be born?" They huddled together briefly, and quickly their spokesman replied, "In Bethlehem, O King. As the prophet wrote, 'You, O Bethlehem in the land of Judah, are not least among the clans of Judah, for out of you shall come a ruler for my people Israel.' It is in David's city that he will be born, O King."

Satisfied with their answer, he dismissed them. To be honest, they looked relieved to get away from the king when he looked so angry. Now he looked a bit calmer, and he began to quiz us. How certain were we about this new-born king? Was it possible we were mistaken? Might it be the king of some other nation? How long ago did we first see the star? I got the impression that he was relaxing, less concerned. I won't pretend I was at ease, because I had already seen once how his temper could flare in an instant, and I sensed that none of his servants trusted him either.

He actually smiled at us. "Go to Bethlehem, like they said. Go there, and search for this child. Make certain that you have found the right child, this 'King of the Jews,' as you called him. And when you have found the house, be sure to come back and tell me. Then I can also go down to Bethlehem and worship him. Now, go; and be quick about it." Despite his smile, I felt uneasy about it.

Anyway, we went out, loaded the camels and got on the road to Bethlehem. Would any of those priests, those men who knew that their special king was to be born in Bethlehem – would any of them be making the journey? There was no sign of them. After Herod had sent us on this mission I had the impression it must be a great distance, much too far for him to consider making. So it was a surprise to find it took us only an hour or so from Jerusalem. It was a relief to get away from the palace with its air of menace. Once we were clear of the city, joy of joys! – there was the star, right ahead of us. And as we approached Bethlehem, the star was directly over the town. It looked as if it was hovering right over one of the houses.

We went to the door of the house, and knocked. My pounding heart-beat sounded louder to me than our knock on the door. In a few moments a little girl answered the door. We asked her if a baby boy had been born here recently, and she told us that a man and a woman were there with a baby boy. This was surely what we had come for. She led us through to meet them.

9

I was so thrilled to be there, and to set eyes on this baby– this King, for whose sake we had made the long journey – that I scarcely noticed any details of the room. I saw the parents, of course, and nobody else there. But I honestly couldn't tell you what the room looked like; I only had eyes for this child. I was over-awed. Would it sound foolish, to tell her why we had come, all about the star and about the king in Jerusalem? Would the words of the prophet be meaningful for her, as they had proved to be for us? She hung on our every word. It clearly did not sound fantastic to her, but the occasional knowing glances to her husband hinted that she was not surprised by what we told them. She was making a real effort to hold onto every little word we spoke. They were full of significance for her. From the way she was dressed, and the simplicity of this unassuming house, I doubt that she was a princess, yet this son of hers was King of the Jews.

They told us that his name was Jesus. They had seen an angel (not a star for them) who had given the name. It meant that he was to save his people from their sins.

Overwhelmed, we instinctively knelt before him, oblivious to what it might do to our robes. Love and joy were welling up inside me, and I whispered, "Thank you, God." Part of me wanted to burst into song – but you know what my singing is like; I didn't want to terrify the baby. Another part of me wanted to ask God to protect this little baby, but I fancied that somehow that was going to happen anyway. Even that vile man Herod would not be able to harm him. We handed over the gifts that we had brought all that way. To explain our choices suddenly became almost impossible: I hope that eventually it will make some sort of sense to her and to the baby.

It was late in the day, so we found a place to stay. I soon fell asleep, full of wonder at everything that had happened in the course of that day. What a contrast there was between Herod in his sumptuous palace, imposing a reign of terror, and this infant who was born to be their true King, and was lying in so mean a place. As I slept, I dreamt. In my dream I saw a man, a most remarkable man. His face was like that baby's face. He wore a crown, but not of the gold we had brought; rather, it was woven of thorns. He held out his hands as if a priest giving his blessing, and in those hands were gaping nail-holes. Perhaps our gifts of frankincense foretelling a priestly ministry and myrrh connecting with death were not so far-fetched after all. He spoke. "Herod will seek to destroy you, and the baby and his family," he said. "You must avoid Jerusalem on your journey home."

We headed south, before venturing east again. I think that even without the warning in the dream I would not have relished another meeting with Herod. As we travelled home we talked endlessly about the baby, and all we had experienced. Perhaps, when he enters his kingdom, this King of the Jews will remember some Gentiles who also came to worship, and find room for us in his Paradise. Perhaps, one day, we shall worship him again, and many will join with us.

CHAPTER 3

An Inquisitive Neighbour

Please don't think I'm being nosy, but my husband does like to know what's going on. If he doesn't know what's what he gets awfully agitated. I had to wake him the other night and let him know all about my cousin – her that's married to the farmer. She found out that she had lost one of her rings. She had to sweep high and low to find it. She was moving cupboards, lifting the mats, under the beds. She even tidied her son's bedroom. It's much too early for spring-cleaning. I told my husband that I'm not starting that for another few months. It took her all day to find it; but she was so pleased when she found it that she had to have all her neighbours in to celebrate. You see what my husband's like? He needed me to tell him that in all the detail in the middle of the night, when we should have been asleep. No wonder he was tired and grumpy the next day!

Me? I'm not that bothered, you know; but I need to find out for him, you see.

That's why I've popped round. I wouldn't disturb you otherwise, but he wants to know. You were just going to make a cup of tea before you go out? How nice – yes, I will join you; even though I mustn't stay long. And if you're having some of your special sponge cake I might be able to manage a little piece.

I can't stand gossips, can you? Not like her down the road. She's for ever inviting herself in, wanting to know everything that's going on, so she can tell the whole town. Model of discretion, me! Keep myself to myself, and don't stick my nose in where it doesn't belong.

Now, you were going to tell me about those visitors you had. I couldn't help noticing them. Mind you, you do seem to have had a lot of visitors just lately. There was that couple who arrived from up north: she shouldn't have been travelling in her condition, and so young. It was good of you to take them in, and just in time. What a place to have your baby! But the little boy looked healthy enough when I saw him. Doesn't look much like Joseph, does he? I wonder what he will be when he's older.

You had hardly got over that when the shepherds arrived, had you? There they were, in the middle of the night – not that I was looking, like. Still, when there's all that noise you need to take a look round the curtains. "What's all that noise?" I asked my husband. "You'll have to get up and have a look," he replied. I told you he was nosy, always needing to know what's going on. He's better than a newspaper for finding out the comings and goings. We heard them arrive, and we heard them go. They were singing their hearts out, praising the Lord.

Next day the story was all round the town. Everybody wanted to know all about it. What with the bright lights, and all the singing. The shepherds said they had seen a choir of angels who told them about a new-born baby who had come to save us. This child was the Messiah, and they would recognize him because he was wrapped up and lying in a manger. That's why they came in such a hurry, and were telling everybody about it. My husband says that if the angels wanted the news spreading quickly they should have come and told me – cheeky monkey!

Anyway, they were right about a new-born baby boy, weren't they? But, you know that already; after all, it was your stable they were in. Better to give birth there than out in the street, I suppose. You will have to tell me the whole story, from beginning to end. My husband will want all the details, and I can't disappoint him, can I?

Yes please; just a little bit of sugar.

It's these mysterious visitors from the east who have got me intrigued. Don't get me wrong – it's my... Yes, dear; that's right: it's my husband who wanted to know... Now, me; make anyone welcome. It takes all sorts to make the world. They can come down from Jerusalem for all I care. But these were *different*. Funny clothes and posh manners – and those camels! Did you notice that they were this year's model, with all the latest accessories? Didn't use maps to find their way – said it was something up there in the sky that told them the way. I never take much notice of these gadgets, but my hus... well, *someone* pointed it out to me.

It was like having a royal visit, wasn't it? We should have put the red carpet out for them, and swept the streets, and got the mayor to welcome them. Mind you, if that King Herod ever comes down here you want to keep out of the way. He's bad news is that Herod. He may be building us a fine Temple, but he doesn't behave like a man who wants to obey God, or sincerely worship him. Some people even say that it's safer to be his dog than his son. I'm sure I wouldn't want my son caught up with King Herod.

All three of them looked like kings. We don't get many like that round here, sat up on their camels. Eh, you got some admiring looks (and some jealous ones) with those parked outside your house last night.

Distant relatives, were they? Just dropping in on their way to somewhere special? Oh, not that visiting you isn't special.

They aren't your relatives, then? And not your husband's either?

We have all had to do our bit of Bed and Breakfast with this census thing, but you don't advertise out in the east, do you?

OK, so why did they call to see you?

It wasn't you they came to see. It was the baby. They were looking for a baby who was the King of the Jews.

No: don't tell me! Let me guess. They saw an angel, who told them to travel all the way here to Bethlehem. They were too late to find him in a manger, but they found him in your house all the same.

No? So how did they find out? Why did they make this long journey?

You're kidding! They had seen his star (he's got his own special star, has he?), and it led them all the way here! So that's what they meant by a thing in the sky to give them directions, and I thought it was a Satnav.

Now you have got me really curious. They came to see the baby, and they came from lands in the east, and they were led here by a star. I've got it right so far? That means we are talking about a special baby – five-star special? All right, one real star; but still, we are talking about a very special baby. I suppose that makes him the star. Pardon my little joke.

You were telling me about them, and there I go interrupting again. So what happened when they came in and saw the baby? Bowing and scraping, and "Yes, your majesty," and all that, was it?

They knelt down and worshipped him. A bit OTT, don't you think? Aren't we meant to worship only God? Even when you make allowances for them being 'foreign' and perhaps a bit ignorant... No, I expect wise men aren't actually ignorant. Even so, to *worship* him is a bit extreme, don't you think?

Mm, your sponge cake is good. Have you offered any of it to Mary and Joseph? Or is it some you had left over from the visitors?

They brought gifts, as well? So what did they bring? Some nice cuddly toys for the baby, and some fragrances for his Mum? One day he'll be old enough for a train set and a bike. Babies always love their cuddlies, and after her journey Mary will want some pampering.

I'm wrong again, am I? She isn't going to smell very nice with frankincense, is she? And what will she want with embalming fluid?

You're saying that they were for the baby and there was nothing for his mother. That makes even less sense. The gold may come in useful, though. Can't go wrong with gold for a king, but I would have thought that frankincense was more suited to a priest offering sacrifices. As for myrrh, that tends to be used at burials – hardly what you give a new-born baby.

Do you think that they know something about this baby that we don't?

The more you tell me about him, the more I want to find out. The angels tell the shepherds that he is Messiah. They tell them that he is a Saviour, and that is good news for all the world. These wise men from the east tell us that he is going to be a king, yet they worship him like God, and bring gifts as if he is a priest. There must be an explanation for it all.

What are they calling him? Joseph, like his father? Jesus. Jesus; yes, that's a nice name. It means 'God will save us' or something like that. It fits what the shepherds were saying, doesn't it? And a nice touch, if he is going to be a king; like those men from the east were saying about him.

With all these angels turning up out of the blue, and the stars in heaven directing foreigners, it certainly sounds as if God has been a bit busy recently. Maybe he is going to save us. Maybe this baby will have a special part to play.

Oh yes; I meant to ask you. How heavy was the baby? My husband will be dying to find out.

CHAPTER 4

One Morning at the Lakeside

Have you ever had one of those days? Nothing has gone right, no matter what you tried or how hard you tried. In fact, it wasn't just that nothing went right; it seemed as if quite a bit had gone wrong. I had a day and night like that; but in the end, everything changed. Let me tell you about it, if you can spare a few minutes?

I've worked round here all my life, just like my father – and his father before him. Trades tend to run in the family, and we're no different. When I was a little lad I would watch him, and long for the day when I could go out with him. Mum, however, was certainly not going to let me stay up all night, so I had to wait until I was older. Long before they let me go out with him I had learned many of the skills. I knew how to guide the boat, whether with the sail or the oars. I knew how to cast the nets, and I knew about cleaning them, to get rid of all the weed that gathered on them. Then we checked them over carefully to see if any holes needed repair. Andrew and I were into our teens before we were allowed to spend the night out on the lake. At first, if I'm honest, I wasn't much good at it. Dad said I made too much noise, splashing the oars and throwing the nets the wrong way. But you learn quickly if your livelihood depends on it. If you don't get a catch that you can sell, you starve. And I had a wife and son to support. We quickly improved, and Dad gave us more and more responsibility. He was gradually handing the work over to us, and to some of the employees.

I don't know what it was that night, but we caught absolutely nothing. Usually, even on a bad night, you pick up a few fish. The lake is teeming with them. Sometimes as you look down it's like a sea of silver, as they dart around. But that night: nothing, nothing at all. Whether the moon was too bright, and the shadow of the boat drove them off, or there was some predator around, I don't know. We tried everything we knew, and all to no avail. By the time the sun was creeping over the hilltops we knew it was no longer worth trying, so we headed for the shore. Feeling cold and fed up, we dragged the boats

19

ashore, and then it was the tedious business of checking the nets. At least when you have taken a good catch you feel it is worthwhile. That morning the tedium just added to the frustration. You could tell the others were feeling the same way. There wasn't the usual banter, the exchanging of jokes or gossip. Most of the conversation was grunts and being snappy at one another. I guess it would have continued like that until we slunk off home for a bit of shut-eye, until Jesus came.

Now I had seen him once or twice before. We had been really excited when John the Baptizer had come. He was telling us all that we needed to get ready because Messiah was coming and God's Kingdom would begin. We needed a change of heart, to put God first. Then, one day, as he pointed at Jesus he said to us, "There! That's the Lamb of God, the one who takes away the sin of the world." It was such an odd thing to say that we couldn't forget it. I mean, there wasn't a sheep in sight; I could only see Jesus.

Then, a few days later, our Andrew said to me, "Come along – I've got someone who wants to meet you." I was intrigued, and followed on. This 'someone' turned out to be Jesus. Straight out, without any introductions, he said to me, "So you're Simon, are you? Well, from now on you're going to be Peter. You'll be a rock." Jesus certainly leaves you plenty to think about, because he didn't explain what he meant by that either.

Come the Sabbath, we went along to the Synagogue, as dutifully as usual. To tell you the truth, I wasn't expecting anything very inspiring – there rarely is. But that morning, Jesus arrived. He was invited to read the Scriptures, which he did. They quite came to life, the way he read them. He was just starting to talk when there was a dreadful commotion. A chap I'd never seen there before began to shout and scream. "I know who you are, Jesus of Nazareth!" he yelled. "Have you come to destroy us?" The more he ranted the more frightening it became. But Jesus was calmness personified. Not the slightest bit ruffled. There was tremendous authority in the way he ordered the man to be silent and the evil spirit to come out of him. The chap was thrown to the ground, with one last scream and convulsion. Then he staggered to his feet, looking totally bewildered. Now he was quiet, docile; no more yelling, no more flailing his arms around in that terrifying manner. If we had not seen it with our own eyes we would not have believed that anyone could simply give the command and a wild man be tamed in an instant.

So, when Jesus came along the lakeside that morning I knew who it was. There were a few of our neighbours in tow, and he sat down to teach them. They hung on his every word. A few more gathered, and within a short time it seemed as if half the town was there. Folk at the back were pressing forward. Just as I was thinking to myself, "The ones at the front will end up in the lake at this rate," Jesus called to me: "Can I borrow your boat for a little while?" He climbed in, and told me to push it out a few yards from the water's edge. From there he could hold their attention while he taught them, the waves gently lapping against the boat. He told them simple stories, like I'd never heard before. He explained the scriptures that we read in the Synagogue, and it felt as if they were speaking directly to us today. He told us how God loves us so keenly, and wants us to become part of his brand-new kingdom.

At first I paid little attention. I was still bad-tempered after the wasted night. I was bored with mending the nets, though I knew the job needed doing. It's the sort of mindless task that allows your mind to wander, and I could not help hearing what Jesus was saying. Somehow, I found myself listening to him. Everything he said rang true. It was as if he shone a searchlight into my heart, and some of what I saw was not very nice. I'm not as good as I like to imagine, after all. My conscience was playing up and I was getting more and more uncomfortable. It felt as if everything he said was addressed to me. I know I don't match up to my own standards; but it was an unpleasant realization that I was nowhere near what God wanted me to be.

Eventually he dismissed the crowds. They had been with him a long time, but nobody had drifted away. They clearly loved every word of it –but not me. I was left very uncomfortable.

As the last of the crowd went home I prepared to get the boat onto dry land. Part of me was relieved that he would no longer be pricking my sore conscience; but another part of me was fascinated, wanting to learn more about this teacher.

But no: he told me to take the boat out into the deeper water. "Now," he said, "cast your nets into the water." It was all wrong. You won't catch fish at this time of day. They're resting, away from the burning sun. Anyway, I'd been out all night and caught nothing. What does he know about fishing? A carpenter, isn't he? Me; I've been involved in fishing as long as I can remember, so I should know. All those thoughts raced through my mind. But in his voice there was that same note of total authority that we had heard in the synagogue. I just knew that, however crazy and illogical it was, I had to do it. They would all think I was a fool, but I had to do it. I cast the net over the side of the boat, just to humour him. To my enormous surprise, almost immediately I felt a tug on the strings. The nets were full, even though it was totally the wrong time of day to find fish. I called to Andrew, and to James and John who were near by. They came and helped pull the net into the boat. We were as open-mouthed as the fish, slithering and squirming in the bottom of the boat. Rarely had I had a catch as good as this. Yet in a moment my mind turned away from the fish, away from the money I would make selling them; it went back to the strange authority Jesus had as he spoke. It played over some of the things I had heard him saying a few minutes earlier. This man disturbs me. He makes me face uncomfortable truths about my heart. If he knows where the fish are, and if he can free a man in the grip of an evil spirit, does he also know the secret, ugly things in my heart? I blurted it out, "Depart from me – leave me alone. I'm just a sinner."

I stared at my feet. I knew that he was still standing right in front of me. He hadn't budged, and he wasn't going to. Very slowly and reluctantly I lifted my gaze, hardly daring to look him in the eye. I was embarrassed; he had shown me an enormous favour, and I was telling him to clear off, without a word of thanks. He had been telling the crowds that God offers sinners forgiveness and new life, and while admitting I was a sinner I was also driving away the hope of a fresh start. When I did bring myself to look in his face, I was surprised to see a warmth and a gentleness. There was a reassuring smile, as if he understood all the turmoil in my heart and wanted to set it at peace. "Don't worry," he said. "From now on you are going to be catching men. If you will follow me, I'll make you into a fisher of men."

Now that's another puzzle to put alongside that 'Lamb of God' business. But, you know what? I think I might follow him, and see if I can make some sense of it. I suspect that before I understand it, he will have made something more of me.

CHAPTER 5

Let Down by my Friends – Thank God!

It's been a long time, so long that I can't rightly remember. Yes, there was a time once when I dared to hope for a cure. In the night I would imagine that my legs were twitching, that I could move them. I might dream that I was walking in the hills, or running with the children. I remembered how I used to swim in the lake, and then dry off in the warm sunshine. I would savour every moment of freedom and movement; and then I would wake up. Obstinately, as if to mock me, my legs refused to move.

Days, weeks, months, years passed by. The hope only grew fainter. I was resigned to being like this for the rest of my days. I could no longer work. I was dependent on the charity of family and friends, and was reduced to begging in the street, whenever I could persuade them to carry me out there.

I lost my dignity. I lost my sense of worth. Life feels a whole lot different when it's only the dogs and the little children who can look you in the eye. In time I lost my sense of shame, as I cried out for money or food. "Spare a coin or two for a poor cripple!" "Give some of your food for a man who's starving!"

Some of the folk took pity on me, while I'd hear others muttering behind their hands. "It serves him right." "He's only got himself to blame." What did they know? Did it matter? Whether or not it was my fault wasn't going to change my condition, or put the clock back. Neither was it going to supply me with the food and clothing I need, just like anyone else.

At evening, friends carried me home. I'd sit there in the darkness, counting up the few coins I might have been given, or trying to make a half-decent meal from scraps of food. I longed for one of them to invite me along to their home for a proper meal, to enjoy human company, and interrupt the monotonous loneliness. There, on my own, alone with my thoughts, I was tempted to wallow in self-pity, or to burn with resentment at the rotten set of cards I had been dealt. I was angry with God. Did I deserve this? Was I to bear this as a punishment for ever? And then I wondered if God was punishing me further for harbouring thoughts like these. There was no escape; I was trapped in this vicious circle that I had constructed.

Occasionally, as I sat by the roadside, I might catch snatches of conversation from the people who walked past and ignored me. They seemed to think that because my legs were useless, so were my ears. Or perhaps, that if they didn't bother to look at me, I would not see them. Out of sight, out of *their* mind, seemed to be their attitude.

You heard them talk about ploughing and sowing and harvesting, in the fields where I used to walk or play. You heard fishermen talking about what they had caught – or grumbling about what they hadn't caught – out in the lake where I used to swim. Sometimes you heard them talk about their children, and the plans and hopes they had for them as they grew up. What work or trade was he going into? Who was she going to marry? No chance that I might have a wife and children, for me to cherish such hopes! And everybody complained about having to pay so many taxes, especially when it's one of our own (that wretched Matthew) who collects them for the Romans and pockets the profits he makes.

I began to hear talk about a newcomer to Capernaum. They called him Jesus, from Nazareth. I tried to piece together the snatches of stories I kept hearing. Some were about him in the synagogue, where he had been teaching. Most of them reckon he's a big improvement on the rabbi; though that was not what they were chattering about. They say there was a madman in there, kept interrupting and shouting out; and Jesus simply told some evil spirit to leave. For a moment, the man screamed and convulsed, and then he lay on the floor quietly, before he stood up calm and normal. It's a strange power, if that's what he did.

Others were telling about crowds of sick people who came to the house where he was staying. He spent time with each of them. He prayed for them; and it sounds as if every one of them was made better. I don't know whether that's true, but I'm sure I'd have liked to find out. It's a shame nobody thought to take me, and see if Jesus could help me.

Over the next few days and weeks those thoughts kept coming back to me. I would imagine the scene in the synagogue, and a man who had such strange authority. I'd try to think what it was like to listen to a man who made sense of God and life. I dreamt of all those sick people turning up at his door, and all going home perfectly well. I pictured myself among them. And every time I started to think like that I got churned up, feeling more and more sorry for myself. I had to pull myself together. It wasn't going to happen; but what if Jesus did come this way again? What if he stopped by me? Would he be able to help me? I scarcely dared to mention these thoughts to anyone, in case they thought I was mad. Truth to tell, I was desperate.

Time passed, and still they were talking about Jesus; but where was he? He was in town! He was here, in Capernaum! As the rumour spread, so I saw crowds scurrying off to the house they said he was in. Oh, how I wanted to run with them!

To my amazement and joy, the chaps who carried me out into the street to beg came along. They said that they were going to see Jesus and listen to him – did I want to come with them? Did I? Did I! They lifted me onto the stretcher, and we lurched along the road quicker than was really safe.

As we turned the corner they paused. What was wrong, I asked. Crowds, they told me. It was packed. There were folk jammed into the doorway and spilling out into the street. We will never get near enough to see or hear him.

Hot tears of frustration and anger welled up in my eyes. Was there nothing they could do? Surely folk might step to one side for me? Before I asked the question I knew: most had never given me a thought in years, so why should they bother now? How cruel it was to have my hopes raised for a moment, and then dashed because we could not get those last few yards.

Suddenly one of my friends exclaimed, "I've got it. I know what we can do – come with me." They had no choice, and neither did I, since I was still on the mat they had used to carry me. Round the side of the house they went, to the steps leading up onto the flat roof.

27

"Hold on a minute, guys," I said. "You can't take me up there. I'll slide off the mat on those steep steps." They took no notice, and I had to cling onto the sides of the mat as tightly as I could. I got a good view of everyone staring at me in sheer bewilderment. It did nothing for my nerves, though I ruefully reflected that if I did fall off, since I was already paralysed, my condition would be no worse. It was an odd crumb of comfort.

I still had no idea how this was going to help me. Jesus was in the house, not up here on the roof. If we had not been able to get into the house, then how was he going to get out, and come up here?

They laid me down, near the small parapet of the roof. It was the nearest I had been to comfort or safety for a little while. Then the four of them started ripping the roof to pieces. I used to be a builder, so I knew how they are made. We would use rushes or branches from trees, and coat them with mud, to bake hard in the hot sun. They are strong enough, and reasonably waterproof, but it's not difficult to dig through them (or to repair them). With a large hole in the roof we could now hear Jesus, and with a little effort we could see him too. But I wanted more. Having got this near, I wanted to be healed.

My friends had another surprise in store for me. They picked up the mat again, and carried me over to the hole. Though I protested, there was nothing I could do as they lowered me down, right into the middle of the crowd in front of Jesus. I yelled at them to take care not to drop me. As I got nearer the floor I saw the puzzled look on people's faces, and a great big grin across the face of Jesus, even as he brushed bits of the dried mud out of his hair.

Now what, I wondered. And Jesus spoke to me:

"My son, your sins are forgiven."

It's not quite what I had in mind. I had hoped he would pray for me, lay his hands on me and pronounce a blessing – something like that. Then I was going to stand on my feet for the first time in years; and it hadn't happened. Did he mean that my sins were the reason that I was paralysed? Or that unless my sins were forgiven, then healing my body might not change much?

Some of the crowd were muttering. "Who does he think he is, forgiving sins? Surely only God can forgive sins – this is blasphemy." I didn't care; but I saw my last chance of being healed about to be snatched away in their arguments.

Jesus spoke again. "Tell me," he said, "is it easier to say, 'Your sins are forgiven,' or 'Stand up and walk'?" While they were weighing it up in their minds, I knew straight off what the answer was. It's simple to say that sins are forgiven, because by the time that gets put to the test at the great Judgment Seat of God, it's too late to change anything. But to tell a paralysed man to stand up and walk – well that can be put to the test immediately. He let it sink in for a few moments, and then he spoke to me again.

"I'll prove to all of you that I have authority on earth to forgive sins. Stand up. Pick up your mat, and go home." You could have heard the proverbial pin drop.

I felt a flood of warmth surge through my legs, almost burning. I felt that same feeling I had known only in my dreams, that I could move my legs once again – but this time it was real, and not a dream. Cautiously, I stretched out my legs, and they moved! I bent my knees, until my feet were flat on the floor. Someone took me by the hand, and helped me to stand. It was so peculiar, seeing the world from this height again, after so many years at ground level. I wanted to laugh for sheer joy and relief, and Jesus laughed with me. "Go on," he said. "Go home in peace. You have really been healed."

To say Thank You seemed so pitifully inadequate that I was quite unable to get any words out at all. But I think Jesus knew the love and gratitude in my heart. I stopped for a moment, and then bent down to roll up my mat. I tucked it under my arm, and made my way out of the door. The crowd parted to let me through. Now I didn't mind how they stared at me, because Jesus had healed me. If they wanted to see what he can do, then let them look at me, I thought. I heard some of them saying, "Praise God; give him the glory," and that was what I felt too.

I glanced back, and saw Jesus still smiling, as if he shared my joy. And then he turned back to the crowd who were still packed around him, and began speaking to them.

I skipped for joy down the street as I made my way home. Those words from the prophet came into my mind, about "the lame man can leap like a deer" when Messiah comes. Had that day arrived? What did that mean about Jesus?

I paused for a moment at the spot where I used to beg, and poured out my heart in love and praise to God, because I would never need to be there again. I looked at my mat, and thought about how often it had carried me for years, and now I was carrying the mat.

Life was starting all over again for me. I was healed; and I began to realize that I was forgiven as well. Everything, absolutely everything, had been forgiven, because he said so. And I wasn't going to mess up this second chance that Jesus had given me.

CHAPTER 6

A Sinful Woman Forgiven

It's a step I have wanted to take for ages. How could I make a clean break with my past? I had grown to hate what I was doing, but could see no alternative. I had grown to hate and despise myself for what I had become.

In my teens I reckoned I was quite attractive – most of the boys seemed to think so, anyway. Truth to tell, I rather fancied several of them too. One night, when we had all had too much to drink, we got too intimate with each other... and it was the first step on a downward spiral. For all that I was ashamed of what I had done so easily, I have to confess that I enjoyed it too. And when my father heard about it I was sent away from home. "You have disgraced yourself. You have disgraced your mother and me. As far as I am concerned, you are no longer my daughter. Goodbye."

Thrown out from home, and nowhere to go, I drifted onto the streets. They call it the oldest profession. Having given way to the temptation once had made it all the easier to give in again – and again. The money was needed, and the more I compromised myself the more it would prove impossible to get respectable work, or find a good man to make me his wife. At first I loathed doing it, and hated myself for doing it; but I felt trapped, as if I had no alternative.

I'm not so attractive now, except if I painted myself up. I looked beneath the surface and knew what a wreck I had made of my life. If only... if only I hadn't been infatuated by the lads. If only I hadn't got drunk that night. If only I had had the guts to say 'No'. Was there any way out? Was there any way back? Was there any way of becoming the person I ought to have been?

For months I wrestled with this thought. Even when I was stood on street corners it would not go away. 'You were made for something better than this. You hate the person you have become. You made yourself into this; but your real Maker intended it differently.' If only somebody special would help to set me free.

31

Standing there, watching to see if anybody wanted me, I dropped back into the shadows. Coming down the street was Simon the Pharisee. He really fancies himself. He obviously thinks he is one of God's all-time favourites, even while he's looking down his nose at everybody else. I can guess what he thinks of me and the other girls on the streets. 'Holier than thou' doesn't get near it. He was walking briskly home, with quite a crowd in tow.

"What's going on?" I asked somebody on the edge of the crowd, hoping they didn't recognize me.

"Jesus, the Teacher, is going to Simon's home for a meal," they told me.

Now this Jesus is somebody I have heard about. Everything the ordinary people say about him is good, though the Pharisees criticized him. Well actually they seem to criticize all of us. It was the stuck-up ones who felt threatened by him. It made me curious. I wanted to see him for myself. Was he really like they said? An idea began to form in my mind. Now was my chance to see him, perhaps even listen to him. If I could just get near him, I thought.

The meal would be a leisurely time. He was going to be there for hours, and that meant I had time. I ran back to my room, and cleaned off as much of my make-up as I could. This was one time I definitely did not want to advertise myself; though who did I think I was kidding? I checked myself up and down. Quite presentable, without this time drawing attention to myself. Almost as an afterthought I picked up the alabaster jar of sweet-smelling ointment. It was a luxury I saved for special occasions, or – I'm ashamed to say it – special clients.

My heart pounding, I hurried back in the direction of Simon's house. Everybody knows where it is, so posh and luxurious. Needless to say, it is in the best part of the city. Like many of his class he loves to flaunt his wealth, so the eating area was in a shaded courtyard that anyone can wander into. Sure enough, there were folk hanging around who I knew. Some had come to beg, and others hoped for the leftovers. Plenty of those, I guess, looking at the lavish spread. And there they were, gawping like tourists at all the food spread out on the table. Finest fish was there, obviously straight from the lake. The smell of fresh bread was wafting over the courtyard. There were so many varieties of fruit, and the best wine flowing freely: Simon was certainly trying to make a name for himself today.

But I wasn't looking for Simon. Neither was I particularly interested in the food on the table. It was Jesus I was looking for – and there he was! As the chief guest he was sat by Simon. Some of the others I guessed must be his disciples. He was lying, propped up on his left elbow with his feet well away from the table and the food. Yes! It was possible for me to make my way round, and get a bit nearer to him.

Oh, I know my reputation in these parts. 'A woman of the city who is a sinner,' is how they describe me. Even my name doesn't matter to them. My pride went the way of my self-esteem long ago. They say that a prophet can identify a prostitute at ten paces: we shall see, I thought to myself grimly. The one real worry was whether I might be thrown out before I got near to Jesus. Being behind Simon and Jesus they didn't notice me. I listened. Jesus was doing more talking than eating. He told stories of how God looks out for the lost, and I thought how lost I was, and how I had lost my way in life. He told how God is not waiting for sacrifices, but a change of heart.

Tears started welling up in my eyes. Whether he knew it or not, this man was offering me the hope I thought I had lost for ever. Here was the possibility of being set free, of making a new start. Polite, respectable people might reject me; but amazingly, Jesus was saying that God would accept me. Was I hearing correctly?

It's not only my reputation I knew about, you see. I knew Jesus's reputation as well. I have heard the Pharisees with their sneers about Jesus. They call him 'A friend of tax collectors and sinners.' Well, if that is true, then I qualify to be one of his friends. It's about the one qualification I've got left.

I felt an overwhelming flood of gratitude, and something I had completely forgotten during those years on the streets – love. I knelt down by his feet, and as my tears fell on them I saw white streaks in the dirt. My hair was dangling (even if it shouldn't have been), and instinctively I wiped his feet clean with it. They call me a loose woman, but my loose hair was proving useful. He knew all that was going on; they were his feet. Yet he didn't try to stop me. He didn't draw back his feet in disgust. Still the tears flowed. They had been tears of shame, as in the presence of sheer goodness I faced up to the truth of all I had been. And as he let me wash his feet – the job of a household slave – I felt as if he was the one washing me clean. I was clean from all my past. I felt the release, and my tears were now tears of joy. I knew that after so many sordid years I was finished with my life of sin. There: I've used the word. I have been honest about it for the very first time. The excuses are over.

By now his feet were clean. I kissed them. To think, my lips had kissed countless men over the years of my shame. Married men; and I didn't bother how we were wrecking their marriages. Inexperienced youths; and I was setting them on a path of destruction. Foreign soldiers; and I was consorting with the enemy. Every one of them knew just what they were doing. They were just as guilty as I was of breaking the seventh commandment. Now, at last, here was a man for me to kiss out of pure love, with no other motive. Here was a man who was not going to abuse me or take advantage of me. Here was a man who saw me as a woman and not just an object for his lust.

I picked up my jar of perfumed ointment. It had cost a small fortune. Normally I had used it to attract customers. Now I broke it, never to be used again for that squalid trade. I poured that sweet-smelling perfume all over his feet, massaging it in because they looked so tired. As the scent filled the air I knew that I had given up my old way of life. It was broken now, gone for ever. It would be as easy to put the fragrance back in the broken bottle as for me to go back to my old life.

I don't know how long I gazed at those feet, the feet made clean by a penitent's tears and wiped by a sinner's hair. Eventually I looked up. I wanted to look into his eyes. I knew they must be the warmest, kindest eyes in the whole world; eyes like I had never looked into on any man's face before. As I lifted my face I saw instead the look of cold contempt, on Simon's face. He recognized me, and was horrified that I was treating his guest this way. An icy fear gripped my heart. It was the awful moment of exposure I had been dreading, of total humiliating condemnation.

But the voice that spoke was not Simon's. It belonged to Jesus.

"Simon," he began. "I have something to tell you."

I wondered if he had another of his wonderful stories up his sleeve. I didn't have to wait long to find out.

"Once upon a time, there was a man who was owed money by two of his friends. One owed him five hundred, and the other owed him fifty." Generous man, I thought, trying to do the sums. The first one owed more than my father used to earn in a full year. The other was going to take quite a time to pay it off, even if it was a lot less. I wondered where this story was going.

"Neither of them was able to pay it back, so he cancelled their debts." Wow; that's not the way the world is. After all these years my Dad has still not forgiven me; and Jesus hadn't finished. He asked Simon a question.

"Which of them will be most grateful? Which will love him more?"

It's obvious, a no-brainer, I wanted to tell Simon. Even I can work that one out.

He was looking for a catch, but in the end he said, "I *suppose* it will be the one whose debt was bigger. He owed most, so he will be more pleased."

"Got it in one," said Jesus. "You have the right answer."

Well, I thought, that was easy. It was terribly obvious. But what was he meaning?

Then Jesus looked at me, and he looked back at Simon. He stared at Simon so long that Simon began to blush. "You see this woman?" Simon nodded.

"You remember when I arrived at your house?" How could Simon forget, considering the fuss he was making trying to ensure that absolutely everybody knew that he had invited Jesus to the biggest and best meal being served in town that day.

"When I got here," Jesus went on, "you did not observe the common courtesies. Nobody bothered to wash my feet, dirty from walking through the dusty streets and tired after a long hot day." Simon shifted uncomfortably. "Now my feet are clean, because she has washed them with her tears, and not with your water." It had not struck me till then, to wonder why his feet were so dirty. Big posh Simon had slipped up on ordinary behaviour.

"When I arrived at your house," Jesus added, "you had no welcoming kiss for me. It did not look as if I was welcome in your home at all." I remembered those long-ago days before Dad kicked me out. Whenever we had visitors he always had a hug and a kiss (on both cheeks) for them. It never mattered whether they were important or not, they always were welcomed that way. What was Simon thinking of that he had not bothered to give Jesus a kiss?

I blushed as Jesus carried on, referring to me. "She has not stopped kissing my feet since she arrived; even though you had no kiss for me. It is polite to anoint your guest with oil, but it's my feet she has anointed with this costly ointment."

Surely Jesus was not giving him a lesson in basic good manners. And what had this to do with the story he had just told? Jesus waited for it to sink in, and then he delivered the punch line. "Isn't it obvious, therefore, that this woman has found forgiveness for her many sins, since she shows so much love? Little loving is a sure sign of little forgiveness."

He looked at me, concentrating as if I was the only person in the world. Certainly he made me feel as if I was the only person who mattered at that moment. Nobody had made me feel like that before; certainly none of the men who had used me down the years. "Your sins are forgiven."

I was so glad he said it that way. He didn't beat about the bush. He didn't talk about 'mistakes', or 'failures'. He didn't tell me I wasn't to blame or offer me excuses. I was a sinner. Whatever other people had done to me, I was responsible for my choices and my actions. He called my life what I knew it was; deep down inside I was sinful. But he had not condemned me for being a sinner. He had just told me straight that my sins were forgiven.

Who is this man, forgiving sins? Only God can do that. The priest can tell you that if you have brought the right sacrifices that will win forgiveness; but I had not brought a sheep or a bull. The peace inside me told me that I was forgiven. I felt what a poet once wrote:

> I did not think, I did not strive,
> The deep peace burnt my me alive;
> The bolted door had broken in,
> I knew that I was done with sin.[1]

I struggled to bring back to mind what I sang in the synagogue in the days when I was still welcome there. "Blessed is the one whose transgression is covered, whose sin is covered. Blessed is the one against whom the Lord counts no iniquity." As the words came back to me I felt the peace. I felt that I was free at last.

Here was a man to believe in. Here was a man who had made me clean on the inside, though I had only made his feet clean. My new-found faith had saved me. I went off in peace, the peace I had wanted for so long.

---

[1] John Masefield *The Everlasting Mercy*

CHAPTER 7

The Raising of the Widow's Son at Nain

I can just about remember the day she was born. I'm a few years older than she is, and my parents lived close by. My younger sisters often played in the street with her, went to school with her. In a small town like ours, everybody knows everybody else to some extent. Generally we know each other's business too, and that isn't always a good thing!

So, of course, we watched as she grew into a young woman. That's when the boys began to take notice, and she was never short of admirers. There was plenty of speculation as to who might win her affection – whoever it was would certainly find himself a fine wife. Of that we were perfectly certain. I suppose she must have been in her late teens – as most girls were – when Joshua shyly but proudly told us that he was going to marry her. Hearty congratulations greeted the news, along with a little quiet envy in some quarters. But nobody was going to get too upset; after all, they seemed so well matched.

The day of their wedding came, and we all turned out to share their joy. The celebrations went on for several days, before they settled into the routine of daily life as a happy young couple. After a while you began to hear some of the older women: "I wonder whether they are planning to start a family." And others, "They're such a lovely couple; they would make brilliant parents." And often it was said just within their earshot. Well, eventually the day came when with a bit of a blush she told us that, yes, she was expecting a baby. More congratulations, and plenty of hugs.

You can't hurry these things. The baby will come in its own good time, and eventually she gave birth to a little boy. They called him Jonathan, the same as his grandfather. "And when are you going to give him a brother or sister?" folk started asking, and she just smiled sweetly.

For all that the question was asked, they never had another child. She rarely talked about it, but you could catch the sense of disappointment. Jonathan was a good lad, a real credit to his parents. His grand-parents (God bless them) would have been so proud of him.

Quite suddenly a shadow came over them. Joshua was taken ill, and within the week he was dead. If I remember it rightly, Jonathan was seven or eight when his father died. She was left to bring him up on her own. Well, we all did our best to help. God's word tells us to take special care of widows, as well as orphans and strangers; but there is only so much you can do, however good a neighbour you try to be. At harvest time we leave the edges of the fields for the widows to glean. We take care not to take all the fruit off the trees, so that there is some left for them. Every little helps, as they say; but some things can't be given them. A boy needs his father, and nobody could take his place.

With help, and a tiny inheritance, she coped very well. Jonathan had his Bar-Mitzvah, and he was growing into a fine young man. Time was coming when he would be able to work, and support his poor dear mother. Of course, most boys start working alongside their fathers, learning a trade and the skills as they do so; but Jonathan didn't have his dad to work with. One of the farmers, who lived just outside Nain, towards Nazareth, offered to take him on. It was a relief to his mother. It promised her a little security, and he worked hard and well.

A day or two back, when he came home, he was complaining of an ache or pain. He thought perhaps he had pulled something, or been too long in the blazing sun. Whatever was the cause, it was proved to be far more serious. He turned feverish, and the next afternoon he died. We wept when we heard the news. She was almost like family to us. Like I told you, we had known her almost since she was born. As a widow she was totally dependent on Jonathan; and now she had been robbed a second time of the men in her life. Her life now was starkly empty. However many years of life remained to her would be bleak and lonely. The dreams she had of grandchildren, of continuing Joshua's line, were taken from her in that instant. Why does God allow such sorrow, such suffering?

At the end of time there will come that great Day of resurrection. All the faithful will rise. Jonathan and his father Joshua will be there. So will those great heroes of the faith like Moses and David, like Abraham and Isaac and Jacob, like a more famous Joshua and a more famous Jonathan. But that is all such a long way off; it is such a remote hope that it gives precious little comfort.

The next day was the funeral. In this heat you mustn't hang on long. Friends and neighbours helped her to wash the body, and to anoint it with spices. They wrapped him carefully in long strips of cloth, and prepared for that last sad journey. He left the house for the final time, carried by four friends on a little stretcher. It seemed as if the whole town gathered to accompany them. At first I could hear the birds in the trees. It felt quite irreverent and insensitive that they should sing so cheerfully at a time like this. Their sound was quickly drowned out as the weeping and wailing grew ever louder. We all felt for her. It was so sad, so tragic. There have been times, I admit, when the crying at burials has just been for show. It was just 'the done thing.' But for them, we felt the pain and sadness so strongly that our tears were genuine. In some measure, it was our loss too.

We passed out of the town gates, onto the road leading north. Ten minutes' walk brings you to where the caves are. That's where most of the burials take place. We won't defile the land in the town with dead bodies, and soil in the country is too precious to use for burials.

We had not gone far beyond the gate when we met a group of men heading towards the town. They were not from Nain, and the leading man looked familiar. And what happened next confirmed why he was familiar. We recognized that it was Jesus, the carpenter from Nazareth. It was what he did that so astonished us, and made us realise it was him.

Instead of stepping to one side to let us pass, he walked up to the bier, so they had to stop. He spoke to the grieving widow. "Do not keep on weeping," he said. How ridiculous! What else was she going to do? Surely she would weep until she had no more strength left in her. Yet, there was something in his tone of quiet, insistent authority. It was matched by such a look of tender compassion in those warm eyes which were fixed so intently on hers. For a moment or two her sobbing paused, and her shoulders stopped heaving.

He took another pace forward, and put his hand on the bier. We were all on tenterhooks. What was he going to do now? Even the act of touching it made him ritually unclean for the rest of the day. In a loud clear voice, that betrayed not the slightest doubt, he said, "Young man, I say to you, arise." You could have cut the atmosphere with a knife. Surely it was the height of madness. A corpse can't hear, can't respond. What a cruel trick to play on this poor widow. The stakes were high. Jesus had a reputation for healing, and people marvelled. Dead men don't rise; so all his credibility was about to go out of the window.

Then, to our utter astonishment, Jonathan twitched, stretched, and sat up. From inside the cloth that was covering his face we heard the familiar voice. "Where am I? What's going on?" Part of me wanted to laugh at such questions. Jesus removed the cloth, and took him by the hand. We saw the face we had never expected to see again. The colour was restored, and he looked the picture of health. Jesus didn't let go, as Jonathan clambered down from the bier, and Jesus gave him back to his mother. She wept again, but this time tears of astonishment, relief and joy.

We could scarcely believe our eyes; though we had seen it from beginning to end. There was no doubting what had happened, no matter how incredible it appeared. There's a psalm that talks about those who sow in tears coming home with shouts of joy. Jesus had turned all the weeping and wailing into joy and praise.

Later on, I knew what it reminded me of. Back in the days of Elijah another widow's only son died. And Elijah restored him to life. But while Elijah performed some sort of resuscitation, Jesus simply spoke the word of command. Is Jesus, then, another prophet, as special as Elijah? Or is he, perhaps, something greater still? One thing is certain, God works through him in a very special way.

CHAPTER 8

The Widow's Son at Nain

"Time to get up! You *are* going to school today, aren't you?" I can still hear it now. I have to admit I was not great at getting up in the morning, except when school was shut, and I was going out to play with my friends. My mum would shout several times – and I would roll over, pretending not to hear. Then she would come in and pull the sheets, and I would have to get up. I'd have a quick bite of breakfast before I dragged myself off to school. Like most teenagers I much preferred sleeping in, and school never held my interest.

"Time to get up!" There she was again, trying to get me out of bed. On Sabbath there was no school, (hooray!); but we did all go along to the Synagogue. No lie-in on the Sabbath either. The three of us would always be there, even if I did earn Mum and Dad a reputation for always arriving at the last minute, or even after the service had started. Occasionally I noticed the rabbi catch my Mum's eye, then glance at me, and raise his eyebrows in despair. Mum must have reacted, because a slight grin would sneak over his face, and a knowing wink as we took our places. Then he continued the service as if nothing had happened. As we listened to the prayers and sang the psalms they drew us into an awareness of God's presence and his care for us. The readings from the Scriptures told us of the great things he had done in times past – even in our part of the land.

"Time to get up!" How embarrassing! They had to wake me up because I had fallen asleep during the rabbi's sermon; and I made sure that *never* happened again: it was rude to him, and humiliating to me. He wasn't a bad sort, and more understanding than I expected him to be. I hear tales of other rabbis who are a lot worse; no sense of humour and no idea about ordinary folk. Mind you, they tell me that there's a new rabbi up in Nazareth who really packs the crowds in. Whether he's in the synagogues or out in the open, they hang on his every word. Mine isn't that good, but I did usually enjoy listening to him (because I made sure not to nod off again!).

"Time to get up!" There was a note of alarm in my Mum's voice. It was still dark, so I knew I wasn't late for school; and the urgency told me something serious had happened. "It's your Dad. He was groaning and had a fever. Then after one big gasp for breath he stopped breathing. I think he's dead." That time I did rouse myself straight away. Although we called the doctor, she was right. He had died; and now there were just the two of us, grieved and shocked. I would have to take on the responsibilities of being head of the house, and bread-winner. Even after the first shock, she was never quite the same – much more anxious, and dependent on me.

"Time to get up! You aren't at school now, you know. If you are late for work they will just sack you." Things hadn't improved as I grew older, and when I got the job on the farm she still had to get me out of bed in the mornings. And now there were no school holidays for me to go out with my friends. But we needed the modest income that it brought, and even then I struggled to get up. I was never actually late for work; but it was a close-run thing a few times. Truth to tell, I quite enjoyed the work. The fresh air was good, except when it rained. At the end of the day you could always point to what you had done, and feel some satisfaction. The farmer was a decent sort of chap too. Provided you did not abuse his generosity he said he didn't mind if we helped ourselves occasionally to some of the fruit while we were working. I could take a little of it home at the end of the day, and the few shekels I earned were just enough to keep us straight. Without that income my Mum would have struggled, I know.

"Time to get up!" I really did not want to. Today it wasn't tiredness or laziness. I wasn't making excuses. I felt dreadful. My legs dragged like pieces of wood, and I was so weak I could hardly lift a thing. By the middle of the day I was sweating dreadfully, and staggering around the place. It was so bad that the farmer sent me home. He told me that if I was in that state I could do no useful work. Somehow I got home, and collapsed into bed. I was so weary I soon dropped off to sleep.

"Time to get up!" My mum was shaking me, to rouse me. "Are you feeling any better? Are you going to work today?" I knew that she was genuinely concerned about my illness; but I also knew how much she depended on me being able to go to work. The income was critical. I could not bear the light, and my head was throbbing, but I tried not to let her see how awful I felt. I clambered to my feet, rather gingerly. Even as I did so I found the room spinning around me. As I fell, I heard my Mum's despairing scream.

"Time to get up!" I felt the tug on my sleeve, and a firm grasp on my hand. I didn't recognize the voice, though. A man's voice; it was gentle, but firm and authoritative. It had the tone that obviously expected to be obeyed immediately, yet without threats or shouting. I stirred. Where was I? What had happened to me? I was lying flat on my back, and could hardly move. There was a cloth over my face, and it seemed as if I was tightly bound. The cloth was taken away, and the situation alarmed me still more. I was out in the open, with crowds all round me. Most of them were crying, wailing, like they do at a funeral. Slowly it dawned on me that I was at a funeral – mine. There was my mother, sobbing her heart out. But standing even closer was the man whose voice I had heard. He was holding my hand, and repeating, "Time to get up!" Was this some sort of dream? Would I wake up and find it was all some grotesque trick of my fevered imagination? I blinked, trying to make sense of anything. "Young man, I tell you, arise!" It was time to get up. The firmness of his voice matched the firmness of his grip. It wasn't a dream. My fever had gone. He wanted me to get up, off the stretcher on which my recently lifeless body had been lying. I sat up, and swung my legs over the side, without any dizziness this time. The men who had been carrying the bier lowered it enough for me to put my feet on the ground. No longer did they feel heavy, needing to be dragged unwillingly along. My strength was returned, with a fresh vitality. I was *alive* – more alive than I had ever been before (if that doesn't sound a crazy thing to say.) As soon as they had untied me I wanted to run and shout and wave my arms –and to say a huge Thank You to him.

There was a look of warmth and friendliness on the face of that stranger. He was the one person there who did not look the slightest bit surprised at what had happened. It was clear that all along he had fully expected me to get up when he told me to get up, even though he – like all the rest of them – knew that I was dead, seriously dead. "Jesus, you are amazing," said someone in the crowd. Jesus! Jesus of Nazareth, that rabbi! I had heard so much about him, and the signs he performed. It never crossed my mind that one day he would touch my life in so special a way. Raising the dead: that doesn't happen every day.

I wonder, I just wonder, because I can't help it, and I've had time to think about what happened to me. When that last great day of resurrection comes, will I hear that same voice again telling me, 'Time to get up!' and will it be that same face of Jesus that will greet me once again with a welcoming smile?

CHAPTER 9

The Woman at the Synagogue

"Ankylosing spondylitis," said the doctor, after he had finished examining me. "I'm afraid it won't get better; it will get progressively worse, and unfortunately there's no cure."

"Ankle what's it?" I replied. "It's not my ankles that are causing the trouble; it's my back. I can't get straight." In any case, he hadn't looked at my feet, so how could he know what was up with my ankles? My back had been painful for months, and I was having more and more difficulty standing upright, with such a curve in my back that I could no longer kid myself it wasn't there. That's when I decided to go and see the doctor.

He repeated it again to me, but slowly – as if I was a bit thick. "An-kyl-o-sing spon-dyl-i-tis," he said. "It's when the joints in your backbone are inflamed, and sometimes the vertebrae fuse together, or they erode in places and grow in others. Either way, your spine gradually locks, your hips become arthritic and it may spread to your knees as well. The ligaments in your back calcify, and that causes the stiffness."

Oh; that's not good, is it?

That was eighteen years ago, when I was in my late teens. I'd felt the stiffness and soreness coming on in my back for a while before I went to see him. I just imagined it would clear up; but instead of getting better it gradually got worse. That's when I went to see him. Well, I can say 'ankylosing spondylitis' now, but I had never heard of it till then. Believe me, I know plenty about it now, and living with the condition. The doctor was right; he could do nothing to help, nothing to heal. I shuffled through my twenties bent double. I looked, and felt, like a little old lady, but not very lady-like.

There's no dignity when everywhere you go you are peering at the floor immediately in front of you. It was a real effort to look up. Imagine, when you meet somebody new, you are looking at their feet and not their face. It takes a massive contortion and twisting to see their face. I stopped trying to see the birds singing in the trees. When we sing the psalm about "I will lift up my eyes unto the hills," in my heart I ache, and wish that I could. Another psalm says "When I look at your heavens, the work of your fingers, the moon and the stars, which you have set in place..." and I can scarcely remember what they look like at all. If someone tells me there's a beautiful sunset, or a bright rainbow, I just have to take their word for it. They don't mean to be hurtful, but it reminds me of what I once took for granted – when I was normal, like everybody else.

What prospects had I of marriage? My best years were spent with my face to the ground. With the best will in the world, nobody would think me attractive – they couldn't even see my face. And there was no chance of bearing children – not like my sisters, not like my friends, who seemed to have hordes of them playing round their feet. I heard their songs, their chatter, their excited screams; and a different sort of silent scream welled up in me. It was another loss, another pain to bear.

Years rolled by – or, should I say, crawled by. The sheer hopelessness of my condition made me more and more miserable. At first my friends tried to sympathise with me, to cheer me up. If I hear another person say to me, "Remember, there's always somebody worse off than you," I will scream so loudly they will never speak to me again. *I* am badly off; isn't that enough? Isn't my condition bad enough to complain?

But wait!

More than half my life has been spent hobbling along, staring at the ground and bent double. I've got so used to it that I'm talking as if it's still like that. And – praise God! – it isn't. Let me tell you all about it.

Although it was never easy, I always made a point of being in the synagogue on the Sabbath. For me, it is part of keeping the day holy. We shouldn't pick-and-choose which commandments to keep. We honour God as we join in worship and prayer. We honour him as we listen to his word. I've told you how some psalms were difficult for me, but I never tire of "As for the saints in the land, they are the excellent ones, in whom is all my delight." If I'm honest, it isn't always terribly inspiring there, but

I need to remind myself that I, too, am one of God's people, and that makes me precious to him.

Each Sabbath I was there. The women are expected to take a back seat, so I was very inconspicuous. The usual folk were there. The farmer with his sons, looking as if he's had a good harvest. The merchant, full of his own importance; he has a splendid nose and he looks down it onto everybody else. I reckon he thinks he does God a favour by coming. Just along the row from me I could see her from the house at the corner. Better than a newspaper for telling you everybody's business, she is. And the widow, God bless her: she's made a good job of bringing up her lads, and she has a kind heart and a gentle tongue. I wish there were more like her.

And there was a stranger, a young man. He must have been distinguished, because the ruler of the synagogue invited him to speak. He read from the scroll, where the prophet tells of a time coming when blind eyes will be open and deaf ears will hear, when the lame will leap and the mute sing for joy. For the lame to leap; that might include me, and it would need a miracle. But it seemed an impossible dream, a picture of a remote and distant time. He began to speak such wonderful words. You sensed that God cared for each one of us personally, and that sometime soon God would reign as king.

Without warning, he stood up. You expect a rabbi to sit while he's teaching. We all wondered what was going on, and didn't have long to wait. He pointed directly at me: yes, me. He told me to come and stand beside him. It wasn't easy, and I had to push past people. What did he want? What was he going to do? I don't like being out at the front, where everyone could see my deformity. Would he tell me that it was my fault, that I must have committed some terrible sins, to be suffering like this? I have heard the whispers; I know that's what some folk think. Trust me, I've searched my conscience often enough, and don't believe I have done anything to deserve this. Other people tell me that if I had more faith, or real faith, then God would cure me. That hurts too.

I thought he was going to say something like that; make an example of me. What a shock when he said, "Woman, you are

49

freed from your disability." That was all. And he was right; I had felt like a prisoner for eighteen years. He put his hands on my head, and then on my shoulders. As he did so, I felt a tingle run down my spine, and a warm feeling that was like stepping out of the shadows into the sunshine. Without thinking, I straightened up. I stood upright, in a way I had quite forgotten how to. As I did so, I could see his eyes. They were friendly and kind. They were piercing, as if he was reading my innermost thoughts, and knew all my secrets. But he spoke not a hint of blame. I shouted God's praise; it had happened just like the prophet had said so many years before. I said my thanks to this kind stranger, this man of God who had such amazing power.

I could look round. Friends were sharing my gladness, and joined me singing God's praise. Then I noticed the ruler of the synagogue. He was stony-faced, and I saw him starting to seethe with rage. "This will not do!" he exploded. "There are six days when work can be done. Come and be healed then; but this is the Sabbath. You are spoiling it." I could not believe it. Surely this was the work of God, and cause for praise.

I discovered that the stranger was Jesus. I had heard that he could heal people, and that he taught with such marvellous wisdom. And now he came out with a wise reply. "You let your animals out of their stalls on a Sabbath. You take them and water them. Should not this woman be allowed to go free on the Sabbath too? She is a daughter of Abraham, and has been bound by Satan for these 18 years." How did he know that?

I felt that my dignity had been restored, and not just my back straightened. I was at last allowed to be 'Abraham's daughter,' and share in the joys and blessings of God's people. My Sabbath had become a rest from my troubles, a share in the glorious freedom of the children of God. The touch of Jesus had changed me, and made me whole, and set me free.

CHAPTER 10

A Shepherd's Tale

I've been getting some grief from the wife; serious grief, I mean. Not just nagging, but serious stuff. On reflection, I think I know what she was getting at, but it all seemed so unreasonable at the time. She just couldn't see it my way, and why I felt like I did. If only she saw it like that she would understand perfectly.

I came in with a few friends – well, when I say a few, it was *quite* a few, actually – and some of the neighbours - I suppose it was most of them, but we've only about twenty or thirty of them. All right, it was all of them. When I told her we were going to have a little party I got the impression she wasn't very pleased.

She was right: I was looking a bit scruffy, just come in from work. Truth to tell, it was more than a bit scruffy. She came straight to the point, in front of all the guests: "You look as if you've been dragged through a hedge backwards!" Little did she know.

Item by item she was taking me to task. "Your cloak's filthy. I can see mud all over it, and grass stains everywhere. And how did it get those tears? And you are no better! I can see cuts and scratches and bruises; there's muck in your hair and on your hands; your feet are filthy and your sandals are even worse. Don't even think about sitting on my best sofa before you've washed and changed!"

She hadn't finished yet, though. "What time do you think this is, to be getting home from work?" I decided it might be wiser not to answer, since I didn't think she really was interested in finding out the time. "You will have spent the last hour or two down at the inn, I shouldn't wonder. Is that where you gathered your mates? And is that where you got into the fight?"

I must confess, it probably did look a bit like that from her point of view. And maybe I should not have expected her to want to throw a party at a moment's notice for all those people, especially since she hadn't catered for them. And, yes, I did look in a bit of a state; but all the same...

When at last she paused for breath, I leapt in with the explanation. "It had better be a good one," she said, almost before I had started.

So I began at the beginning. She knew what a grand day it had been; pleasant and sunny, with a bit of breeze, and not too hot. Really, it was a good spring day; so I decided to take the flock up to the top meadow. The grass is always lush there at this time of year, and the lambs can gambol safely.

I hadn't a care in the world, as I let them out of the fold. I set off up the lane, with the flock following on behind. As we made our way I enjoyed listening to the birds singing in the hedges, and the flashes of colour from the flowers along the way. Some of the sheep were stopping to graze as we went; but I didn't mind greatly. It didn't matter when we got to the meadow, because there was a long enough day in front of us. So long as we got there before the sun was high we would be fine.

Along beside the stream we went, stopping while most of them took a drink. It's safe for them there. The water is shallow, and it doesn't flow quickly. Where it's deep, or fast-flowing, a sheep could be in trouble. If they fall in, their fleece fills up and they can't fight the current; and even if you reach them in time, their water-logged fleece makes them a very heavy load to drag out of the water. Here, by still waters, they were safe. I paddled in the fresh water, washing dust off my feet. As I did so I caught the reflection of their faces – did I just imagine it, or were they also looking at the reflection of their shepherd?

When I judged that they had had enough, and that it was time to move on, I picked up one of the lambs and started to carry it off along the path. It was bleating, and that immediately attracted the ewe, so she came. The rest of them followed – like sheep, I nearly said.

On we went, under the shade of the mountains. Early in the day, especially at this time of year, it is light and inviting. But towards winter time, it has a cold, dark and forbidding feel to it. The valley of the shadow of deep darkness, we call it; and others call it the valley of the shadow of death – I can understand why. But with me taking the lead, the sheep seemed to feel safe enough. An occasional nudge with my staff was all it took to keep them moving, until we reached the meadow.

There was nobody else there. Sometimes other shepherds will bring their flocks – it's big enough for several. Then we sit and tell each other stories. We have to keep half an eye open for dangers, whether from wild animals or robbers. I've not had much trouble, but there are stories of lions and bears that had to be fought off in the past.

An hour or two later my friend Jonathan arrived with his flock. I hadn't seen him since lambing, so I asked how it had gone. "Very well," he replied. "Can you guess how many I have in the flock now?"

I looked round. It was a bit difficult to gauge, what with them wandering around, and mixing with my flock. Still, it looked as if there were more than double what I had brought. "About a hundred and twenty," I guessed. "Not far out," he said, "but actually I have one hundred and twenty four." Typical shepherd, I thought to myself, knowing just the exact number.

"I had a good season too," I told him. "And to make it easy for me I have got exactly one hundred. The last ewe had twins, and that made it the round hundred."

I stopped talking, but I didn't stop thinking. When you live with them, they become almost like friends, or even family. You remember earlier generations and who their mothers were. You watched them take their first steps on spindly legs. You shared some of their joy as they bounced over the green grass. You pulled them out of thorn thickets, and rubbed oil into cuts. You teased out the ticks, because sheep never clean their own fleece. It's little wonder that most of us have pet names for each sheep in our flock. The most recent one of all I called Hephzibah. It means 'My delight is in her.' She really is a little darling, with the cutest markings on her nose. I gazed round the field, and there she was, playing with her twin, while mother kept an eye on them from a short distance. A faint smile crept across my face.

Through the afternoon our flocks carried on grazing. Most of the time somewhere you would see a lamb running to its mother to suckle, its little tail wagging with delight. Elsewhere some were being adventurous and exploring, though never wandering too far off.

I wanted to get them home and into the fold well before darkness fell. It was time to gather them together. A layman might imagine Jonathan and I had an impossible task, sorting out which sheep belonged to which flock. It's amazingly easy for us. I stood a short distance away, and called. All of my sheep came to me. They know my voice, you see, because they have spent so much time with me. When I call, they come. It's different for the hired hands; they don't spend long enough with the flock for the sheep to get to know them. But for us who own the sheep - they come readily enough for us.

I led them back the same way we had come. Inevitably there were stops to drink, and plenty of cropping of the verges as we passed along, but it was well before sunset as we approached the fold. There would be plenty of time for me to check each animal over, removing any thorns or insects, checking them for cuts and looking out for injuries. I sat down by the gateway, and saw the first one in. She was looking fine, so in she went. The second had a few twigs caught in her fleece, but I soon got those out. So it went on; most of them were fine, or needed only a little attention. One or two had minor cuts, but I cleaned those up and rubbed in the oil. It didn't take long before the last one was in. But I had only counted ninety-nine; I was sure of that. I'm always most careful about it, since the sheep are my livelihood. I went into the fold, and counted again. There were definitely ninety-nine, and not one hundred. Check once again: it was Hephzibah who was missing. When you know all of them by name, they matter to you, and you know which one is missing.

People might say I'm soft, but there was no way I was going to leave her out there. The ninety-nine were safe enough in the fold, once the entrance was secured; so I left them there and retraced my steps. Where might she have wandered? Isaiah may not have been a shepherd, but he certainly got it right when he said that "all we like sheep have gone astray, and turned every one to our own way." If they take it into their heads they will wander where the fancy takes them.

I called out to her as I went, and listened for the bleating. Nothing. From long years of experience I thought I knew the likeliest places to look. I scoured the bushes. I waded in the stream. I clambered up the rocks. I looked behind the hillocks. I peered over the walls. I was getting more anxious. Had some animal snatched her while my back was turned? I tried to keep alert as I was leading them, but I had to admit the possibility.

By now the sky was starting to turn red. 'Red sky at night, shepherd's delight,' they say. Well this shepherd had precious little delight right then, I can tell you. I reached the meadow. Jonathan had long since gone with his flock. She would not have gone with them, because they would know she didn't belong. And there was no sign of her anywhere in the meadow.

All I could do was make my way home, still keeping my eyes peeled for any sign of her. As I reached a fork in the track, some instinct made me try the 'wrong' road. Could she have wandered off down there, while the rest of the flock followed me? Then I saw her! There she was, caught in a thicket. She stared at me so pathetically, and so frightened. Her fleece was streaked with blood and there were many twigs in it. She had obviously been tugging and struggling to free herself. I used my staff to part the branches and fight my way into the densest part, where she was caught. The crook came in useful to hold her still, while I tried to free her. Being spring time, the branches were tough, not easily broken, and it took ages to prize her out. By the time I did, I was nearly as exhausted as she was, and I had plenty of cuts to show for my troubles, to say nothing of tears to my clothing.

She was too tired, too forlorn, to walk back to the fold with me. There was only one thing for it. I grabbed her firmly with two legs in each hand, and put her over my shoulders. It was awkward, and with each step she felt heavier; but I could not have left her there.

It was a long walk home, carrying that load on my back. But, tired though I was, I was also rejoicing. My relief as I let her in to the fold was not only at getting the weight off my shoulders, but also that my lamb was back where she belonged. I wanted everyone to share my joy. My lost sheep had been found, and was back where she belonged. Does anyone want to party with me?

(But I had better go and get washed and changed first.)

Jesus said, "There will be more joy in heaven over one sinner who repents than over ninety-nine righteous people who need no repentance."

CHAPTER 11
A Farmer's Widow

I don't know what I shall do without him. It all happened so suddenly, with no warning. Only a week ago we were making plans for a comfortable retirement, and now we're making plans for a funeral. A week ago the question was about where to store the grain, and now it's what flowers to get. A week ago we were singing, "All is safely gathered in" and now it's, "Abide with me."

I can't concentrate – you will have to bear with me. It was all so sudden. There he was, doing his accounts with such a satisfied smile on his face, while I went off to bed. I was a bit surprised that he hadn't joined me, and then a bit alarmed. So back I came to investigate. I found him slumped in the chair, gone; just like that. We had not even been able to say goodbye.

Everything had seemed so good until then. The land he farms – farmed - is so fertile. It has always produced good crops. A year or two back he came in, so proud, and said, "It's the biggest, best crop I've ever had. And it's a lot better than anybody else's for miles around."

"That's good," I said, trying to sound impressed, but not really feeling it.

"I've got a plan," he continued. "I've had such a bumper harvest that I can scarcely get it all into the barn. So, ready for next year, I'm going to tear down the old barn – it was looking a bit tatty anyway – and then I will build a new one, bigger and better. I saw a design I liked in the catalogue. Then you and I should be able to relax and enjoy our wealth."

Well, once he has got an idea like that into his head, nothing will stop him. I learned that a long time back; so I knew to just let him get on with it. Once he had sold off that year's crop he attacked it with his sledge hammer. There were bits of wood flying everywhere, and when eventually he finished he had a massive bonfire. Some of the bits he salvaged to help with the new barn; and I do have to admit that it looked quite impressive, and a great improvement on the old one.

In the spring he was out there in the fields, ploughing and sowing in the rich, dark soil. He watched for the rains coming at just the right time, and for the green shoots to pop up and then fill out to lovely plump ears of grain; and he rubbed his hands with glee as the sun shone on the fields, ripening them into a vast golden cloth. He could hardly wait to harvest it, and get it all into his huge new barn.

The day came, and he was up at the crack of dawn. He had his men out there, and their wives, and their children: all toiling away to bring it in. Sheaf after sheaf they carried to his barn, while he stood there counting them. At midday they took a break from the blazing sun. Sweat was pouring off them as they tucked into their butties and swigged the drink. As it got cooler they went back to shifting the rest of the sheaves. I could see, and I'm certain he could, that even his new barn wasn't going to hold it all. But was he disappointed? Not a bit of it!

"It's a new record harvest," he shouted proudly. "Let's see what they make of *that* at the Farmers' Club next month. I should certainly get the silver cup this year."

"Does that mean I get a new frock for the dinner and presentation?" I asked, suddenly noticing a small silver lining to the cloud.

There was a sudden onset of male deafness. "I know what I am going to do," he went on.

"Surprise me," I said, with an air of resignation.

"I shall pull down the barn, and build an even bigger, even better one."

I was about to ask him what he planned to do after that, but thought better of it. I wanted to call him a fool for pinning all his hopes on another great harvest, but it wasn't quite the done thing. It was all planned in his head. He knew how big it was going to be, how much timber he would need, even how many nails. He was already calculating his profits, and where we could go to spend our retirement.

The year passed, all dominated by this obsession of his to complete this monster of a barn, and to prepare for a harvest that would make all the neighbours green with envy. Sure enough, when it was finished, the barn was a whopper. And just as surely, so was the harvest. There was a real glow on his face as he came in from the fields that day when the harvest was finally in.

"We've done it," he said. "Just like I said we would. That there barn is full to the rafters, and the income from that will see you and me comfortable for years to come. We can take our ease and enjoy life to the full."

"But where does God come into all this?" I asked him, a little hesitantly.

He laughed at me. "I don't bother him, so I don't suppose he'll bother me. Besides, this is all the result of my hard work. Don't you think I'm entitled to enjoy it?"

He often talked like that, and I never liked it. I always had this uneasy feeling that one day God would come knocking on the door – and that night he did.

"Eat, drink and be merry;" that was his motto. It was convenient to ignore how it goes on, about "for tomorrow we die." And that tomorrow came sooner than he bargained for.

Now I've got the worry about all that crop, and he never will get to enjoy it. All those plans and dreams – they're all gone now. I can't enjoy it, not without him. What's the point of being rich with goods, if you are a pauper in your soul? What is a harvest like his worth, if the harvest of your life amounts to nothing?

CHAPTER 12
The Tax-Collector and the Pharisee

I don't have to ask, 'Why does nobody like me?' I already know the answer. Most of them despise me, or even hate me. They call me a collaborator – or worse. But a man has to work; and I have a wife and family to support. There's no charity comes in our direction. And taxes have to be collected. I know some of them go to maintain the Roman governor and his army, and some go to indulge that villain of a king, Herod. Even so, people do want law and order, and that doesn't come cheap. They want public buildings maintained, and that doesn't come cheap either. We Jews have paid the Temple tax for generations, to support the priests and provide the sacrifices and so on; so taxes are nothing new, are they?

I try to justify it all to myself, make it all sound reasonable and fair. Some of the taxation is fair, but I have to admit I don't agree with all of It, though I still have to collect it. What is harder to justify is the Romans' system of farming out the tax-collection. You see, provided we give them all the tax-money that they ask for, they aren't worried how we collect it, and they aren't bothered how much we rake off for our own use. That rake-off is our wages. Well, you can see how easy it is to exploit a system like that, with the authorities turning a blind eye to the less honest methods employed. We can over-charge as much as we like, and make a very handsome income. The drawback, as you can easily guess, is that we don't make friends that way, only enemies. Nobody really likes to pay taxes, and if they see us being too ostentatious with our wealth, or sense that we are getting rich at their expense, I suppose it is not to be wondered at. There are nights when I get very little sleep, my conscience working overtime. There are days when I quite share the contempt that so many of my fellow-countrymen feel for me.

I need to tell you something else, and I don't find it easy. There is much more that my conscience goes to work on than just my work as a tax-collector for the Romans. Oh yes! Now I'm not talking about scandals, what hits the headlines in the gutter-press; and I'm not talking about the sort of behaviour that would have me hauled before the courts if anyone else knew about it. I just have the constant oppressive burden, that I am not the person I ought to be. I know that God is there, and he knows my every thought, my every word, my every deed. I know that in spite of everything he loves me, even when I can't love myself. If he didn't love me he could have wiped me off the face of his earth a long time ago, and his perfect justice would have been satisfied (even if his heart of love would not). I would never be able to plead that he had not been fair.

Occasionally I go along to our synagogue, but I am not comfortable there. Too many people know who I am, and I know they are whispering behind their cupped hands. Tax-collectors and sinners: they always lump us together, and I can hardly say I blame them. They will move, rather than sit near me. More often I will call in at the Temple while I am passing. It's safer, more anonymous, less likely to be recognized there.

Whenever I go, and whether it's to the synagogue or to the Temple, two things particularly strike me. The first is almost an instinct that I cannot explain. I have that strong, deep sense that not only *ought* I to pray and to praise God, but also that he actually wants me to do so. He is great, and he is good; he is kind and he is merciful. The second overwhelms me each time I hear the Law being read. It condemns me, and I cannot escape that. I am guilty before God, and I am guilty at the bar of my own conscience. Like I told you earlier, it isn't that I have been a law-breaker (except the Law of God), and it isn't that I have allowed myself to slip into immoral or deceitful behaviour. I just ignore God too much of the time. I cannot pretend that I love him, or that I delight to do what pleases him. When I hear those words in the Psalms "I delight to do your will, O my God; your law is within my heart," I cringe, because I know it isn't true. It certainly ought to be, but I know that it isn't. When I hear those words "Who shall dwell on your holy hill?" I flinch, because I know the next lines exclude me completely. "Whoever walks blamelessly and does what is right and speaks the truth in his heart; who does not slander with his tongue and does no evil to his neighbour, nor takes up a reproach against his friend... who does not put out his money at interest and does not take a bribe against the innocent." There is no way that I match up to that standard, and the secret thoughts of my heart put me even further from God. I am not fit to come into God's presence. Do you wonder that I feel so wretched and so guilty? When they call me a sinner I can only mumble my agreement.

I wish that I did better. I wish my heart did love God constantly. I wish my life was good and kind and generous. I wish that praises came to my lips as readily as some of the less pleasant words, the hurtful and destructive snapping at those around me. I wish that I kept God's commandments more truly. I wish that I knew his peace in my heart, and had the sense of his smile upon me.

I envy those Pharisees, you know. Everybody knows how virtuous they are. They keep God's laws. They are always praying, or worshipping, or studying his words. All their time is devoted to God, and they take such care to keep even the least of his commandments. You never seem to catch them out, doing or saying the wrong thing. I wish that I was like that.

Why, just the other day I sneaked quietly into the Temple. Of course, I did not dare to go too close. I am not fit to get close to God's holy presence. I had to keep my distance. But one of the Pharisees was there, right at the front, and I could hear what he was saying to God. In fact, I think just about everybody in the Temple courts could hear him, and half of Jerusalem; he was shouting so loud. There he was, reciting all his good deeds, telling God – and the rest of us – how well he keeps God's laws. He fasts twice a week, even though the law only asks for it once; and I don't often manage even once a week. He always remembers to give the tithe, the tenth part of all he has. Me? Well I sometimes give a bit to the poor...

Nobody could imagine him being an adulterer, a thief, or extorting money fraudulently. He even said that he wasn't like other men, and I guess I have to agree with him. Mind you, I thought it was a bit mean to say to God that he *thanked* God that he wasn't like *me*. However much I think it of myself, it did not seem right for him to be saying that.

I stopped still for what seemed a long time, though it might only have been minutes. I weighed up all those thoughts that have pummelled my conscience. I thought about those words from Scripture that had the knack of piercing my defences and challenging my motives. I thought about how far short I fell of the standards of these holy men around me.

I wondered about all those lambs that get sacrificed, only yards from where I was crouched, not daring to raise my eyes towards heaven. I remembered how on the solemn Day of Atonement, the High Priest will come out in his splendid robes. He brings out the two goats, and puts a hand on both heads while he confesses our sins. Then one of the goats is slaughtered, as if to say, 'That is what your sins deserve.' The other goat is led off into the wilderness and released, never to be seen again. It makes me think of those words, "As far as the east is from the west, so far does he remove our transgressions from us." God must be trying to tell us something by this ritual. What if my sins really can be taken away? What if there is forgiveness for a sinner like me? What if God will accept me, and not reserve his favour only for good and holy people? Is there hope, even for me?

I tried to get my head round all these thoughts. I needed to make sense of it. I puzzled over the way that on the Day of Atonement it is the Priest who brings out the goats for sacrifice. At other times, the worshippers must bring their own animals; but here it is as if God is providing the sacrifice for himself. He takes the initiative to deal with sin, which surely must mean that he takes it away. He could hardly refuse to accept the sacrifice which he himself had provided, could he? My sins might be like scarlet, as God said through the prophet; perhaps they may become white as snow. When I stop comparing myself with the Pharisees, and think about the holiness of God, how dreadfully far short of his glory I fall! Yet he has provided a means of pardon. There is hope, even for me. Dare I ask for pardon? Dare I seek mercy? I can do no other, but implore him, "God, be merciful to me a sinner."

Didn't David have to pray like that? I may not have sinned as he did, yet I feel the burden of my sin, my failure to honour God as I ought. If David's prayer was accepted, mine might be also. "Have mercy on me, O God, according to your steadfast love; according to your abundant mercy blot out my transgressions. Wash me thoroughly from my iniquity, and cleanse me from my sin." Surely that covers all! "Create in me a clean heart, O God, and renew a right spirit within me." Yes; I can pray with sincerity, "God, be merciful to me, a sinner."

Even as I say it I feel a weight lifted from my shoulders. I feel a peace flooding into my soul. He has accepted my prayer. Better still, he has accepted me.

CHAPTER 13
A Disturbed Night

Well, I thought that now the kids were a bit older I would not have my nights disturbed. How wrong can you be? Still, the oldest ones will be teenagers soon, so I guess I am getting some good practice for when that time comes. But if I sound a bit grumpy, please bear with me; I hadn't bargained on my night being disturbed like it was.

We're a fairly typical family, I'd say. We aren't wealthy, but neither are we poor. We make a living for ourselves; we grow fruit and vegetables, most of which we eat, but have a little left over to sell. The grapes make good wine, and the olives produce some really excellent oil, though I say it myself. We keep a few animals too. At night, those come into the lower part of the house – a bit of a smell at times, I have to say; but in the winter they produce a nice bit of warmth for us. There's a raised part of the house, where we live and have our meals around the charcoal fire. At night we settle down on mats in the same area. A few blankets cover us, and we keep each other warm – and hope that the symphony of snoring doesn't keep too many awake!

As I said, we are a typical household in these parts. Most of our neighbours are the same. They make their living as we do, pay their taxes like the rest of us and we all grumble about our rulers. We pray together each week in the synagogue, and our children go to school with each other. They play in the street and pop in and out of all the houses. In many ways it's like a big family, but all living in our several houses.

Days pass, and apart from the changing seasons, and observing the rest on Sabbath, life carries on in the usual routine. We try to help each other when there's need. I was grateful to the ones next door when I was ill a few months back. She made several meals for us, and kept our children occupied and out of the way until nightfall. I'd like to think that in the same circumstances I would do the same to help her. And last night I had to! "Any time you need a favour, just ask," I had said, never thinking that she would take me up on it.

It had been a normal day – working, cooking, eating, caring for the animals. We brought them in and settled them down. Brought the children in and settled them down as well. Finally, with all the jobs done, we asked God's blessing on our home and family, kissed each other good night, and lay down to sleep. With all the fresh air and the hard work I soon dropped off. I was ready for a good night's kip. I was well away when I was woken by a hammering on the door. It was still dark, and I struggled to rouse myself. The hammering continued urgently.

"Who is it? What do you want?" I called out – not in the best of moods, I have to admit. I couldn't imagine what was so important that we had to be disturbed in the middle of the night. Was the house on fire? Was someone ill or had somebody died?

"It's me," said the voice. I recognized my neighbour immediately.

"Yes, but what do you want?" I replied wearily.

"Can you help me, please?"

A bit impatiently, I called back, "We are all asleep – or, we *were* until you started knocking so loudly. We are all tucked up and it will disturb the whole family. Is it really that important?"

Further tapping on the door was the answer. There was clearly no chance of getting back to sleep before I had gone to see what was up. I stumbled around, trying to find the little oil lamp, and a flint to light it. I picked my way over the slumbering bodies, muttering, "I'm coming, I'm coming" to try and forestall any more thumps on the door. I thought to myself, "It had better be urgent."

There's a big heavy bar across the door, so I had to lift that and then lay it down. I hoped that the animals wouldn't think that morning had come and go out with me. As I opened the door, there was my neighbour, just about to rap again.

"I'm sorry to trouble you..." I resisted the temptation to say what I was actually thinking.

"So what's the problem?" I asked. In all conscience, it was out of character for them to disturb us like that, especially so far into the night.

"It's like this," he began. "We had gone to bed, like you. I'm really sorry to have had to wake you, but it seemed there was no alternative. That was when my cousin arrived. He was travelling home from Jerusalem, and because night had fallen he decided to stay with us. He had not timed his journey properly, or he would have arrived in daylight, and I would have had food to offer him. Now I know that you usually bake extra bread, and it would be terribly rude of me not to give him some fresh bread. It will take me an hour or two to light the fire and prepare him food. Do you think you could manage a small favour, and let me have a few small loaves?"

By this time I was a bit more awake, even if I was slow in thinking. We did have a few loaves left over from the day just gone, and we could spare them. I could understand his predicament, even if I wasn't best pleased to have been disturbed like that. I knew that I would not be able to sleep if I sent him away empty-handed when all the time I was able to help. And later I reflected that he had paid me a compliment, in a funny sort of way. He had had sufficient confidence in me, and in our friendship, to wake me in the middle of the night with such a request. Even though I did not feel generous, I pitied his predicament and half admired his pleading. I knew where the loaves were, and went to fetch six – not just the three he wanted. I wished him goodnight.

"God bless you, and give you peace," he said. He turned and hurried home. "And thank you, thank you, thank you," he added as he went.

Wearily I closed the door, and put the bar back in place. I was relieved that none of the animals had stirred. By the flickering light of the oil lamp I picked my way across the floor, to find my spot under the blanket again, before snuffing out the lamp. I lay down, but did not get off to sleep quickly. I lay there in the darkness. I could still see the despair in my neighbour's eyes as he had pleaded with me. I sensed the humiliation he must have felt in not being able to provide any food, and how he must have felt about having to disturb me. And that was when I began to feel a bit less resentful, and even a little honoured, that he had enough confidence to come and ask me. Still half awake, I began to pray for my family, one by one, that they would grow up to love God and be thoughtful for other people. I did not make the connection straight away, but slowly the realization came that a few minutes ago I had been called on to live out that same prayer. Every day and every night I ask God to supply our food, to give us today our daily bread – and I expect my neighbour does too – and now I had been the answer to that prayer for him.

I lay silently for a while, and still no sleep came. Then I felt as if a voice, the voice of God, was saying to me: "It's a good thing I don't mind what time you speak to me! You can call on me whenever you want, and I will hear you. You often sing that 'He who keeps Israel neither slumbers nor sleeps.' It's true, you know; I do stay awake and remain attentive. You can knock on my door at any time, but you must keep on knocking, keep on asking and keep on seeking; it will show that you are genuine and that you truly believe I love you enough to answer you. And even if you were grumpy about having your night's sleep interrupted, I am pleased that you didn't turn him away. Good night, sleep well - and *God bless you*!" Perhaps he smiled when he said that.

CHAPTER 14
Nicodemus Reflects

If you had asked me a few years ago if I could envisage myself doing this, I would have laughed at the absurdity of it. Even last week I would have dismissed the idea out of hand. After all, I have a status, a position of dignity (in your time you would probably call me a Professor); people expect me to conduct myself properly. Making myself 'unclean' or 'defiling' myself, is not something that I would consider for a moment. And now I have done it, and I am glad, rather than ashamed. Touching the dead technically makes me unclean for a day, and now that I have done it I have a quiet sense of satisfaction; though I wish it hadn't been necessary. You know what makes it even more peculiar? What makes it even more surprising that I should do it? He had been executed like a common criminal: crucified.

You won't read much about me. I get just three mentions in the Good Book; and this was the third one. After Jesus was crucified, Joseph and I decided to do the last bit we could for him. We asked Pilate for permission to take the body, and give it a proper burial. It was just too awful to imagine his body being thrown into the valley. After the Romans had taken him down we wrapped him in a sheet. Those hands had touched and healed hundreds, and now great nail-holes had torn them. Those lips had spoken such amazing words of wisdom and hope, and now they were still and silent, with ugly bruising all round them. The eyes which once had been so searching, penetrating the deep secrets of our hearts, were now closed. The soldiers had crowned him with thorns, and we plucked out the last of the spikes. There was a gaping hole in his side where a soldier's lance had confirmed that he was dead. How could they inflict such injuries on so good a man?

In the garden close by Joseph had the tomb that he had been saving for his own use. It was a cave, hewn out of the solid rock, with something like a ledge running along one side. We would lay his body there. Custom dictates that the body is wrapped with linen bandages, and spices packed into the cloth to mask the smell of decay. Even though the Sabbath was approaching we brought some 70 pounds of them, and used them all. His head we wrapped in a separate cloth, out of respect. Then we laid the body on the shelf. Very sadly, we paused. We prayed. We thanked God for a man so good, a man on whom we had pinned so many hopes. It was an effort to tear ourselves away, but Sabbath was close, and we must rest from all work.

You may well ask why his family did not do this, or why his closest followers were not there to help. Why did we go to this trouble for a man we weren't related to? Why risk the contempt of other men in the Sanhedrin, by associating with a man they had condemned, and had crucified under the curse of God? Well, for me it goes back a year or two.

Jesus was already gaining a reputation. He was a wonderful teacher, or so they said. He had not been to the rabbinic schools, yet he knew and he understood with such clarity and simplicity. I spent years in study and training. Over the years I gradually earned a reputation as *the* Teacher of Israel. My opinions carried weight, even on the trickiest of subjects. Yet without having had such training, and without having gone through all these studies, Jesus was renowned as a teacher. How could this be? And, they said, he performed signs and miracles. Now I may be a distinguished teacher, and I have certainly studied very thoroughly, but I don't 'do' miracles. But so many people told how he healed the sick, cleansed lepers, restored sight to the blind, set cripples back on their feet; they could not make it up on that scale. One or two, it might be an exaggeration or even a hoax; but not when it was so many. I had to find out for myself, and for the others in the Sanhedrin. After all, they were perplexed by him as well.

One night, under cover of darkness, I sought him out. I hoped nobody would see me, because a respected rabbi like me ought not to be seen with him. I picked my way through the familiar streets to the house where I knew he was staying. There was no moonlight to show me the way, but it did mean there was less chance that I might be spotted. There was not a soul to see. As I hurried along the streets I rehearsed what I wanted to say to him. I would start by acknowledging that he must be a teacher sent from God. It would be foolish to pretend otherwise, and it would show him that I was sympathetic, not hostile – unlike some of my colleagues. Then I would ask him where he got his learning and insight from; perhaps he was inspired like the prophets of long ago. Then I wanted to ask him what he meant by 'the Kingdom of God.' He talked about it a lot, but there are so many different opinions: what did *he* mean? How would it come? Was it coming in our life-time? Those questions would certainly make for a fascinating and illuminating conversation – or so I thought.

He welcomed me, and seemed to know who I was without introduction. I started with the line I had been rehearsing: "Rabbi, we know that you are a teacher sent from God, because nobody can do the signs you do unless God is with him." 'Rabbi' was a mark of my respect for him, even though I knew he had not trained as one; but he clearly had a true authority. I paused for a moment, getting ready for my first question. But without waiting for the question, he took over. It was not what I expected, and it puzzled me.

"Truly, truly, I say to you." (I was to discover that when he had something really very important to say, he often began this way.) "Truly, truly, I say to you, unless a person is born again, they cannot see the Kingdom of God." I had been intending to ask him about the Kingdom of God, but here he was turning it into a riddle. What could he mean by being "born again"? I had never heard anyone use an expression like it.

After all, I am a grown man. Surely he did not mean that I must return to the womb of my dear old mother – God bless her! But what else could he mean? The very idea was grotesque. Going back to babyhood, when my own children are adults: it made no sense to me. Yet he was so obviously in absolute earnest about it. Perhaps he could explain it, make it clearer?

"Truly, truly" (there he goes again), "I say to you, unless you are born of water and the Spirit, you cannot enter the Kingdom of God." Now, as far back as I can remember I have followed God's commands as fully and obediently as I knew how. Was Jesus saying that I needed to 'qualify' for God's Kingdom in a totally different way – in effect, start my life all over again? What did he mean by being "born of water"? Was it anything to do with this practice of baptizing people that had become so popular recently? Normally we reserve baptism for Gentiles who want to become members of our Jewish religion, but John had been telling people that they also needed a change of heart. They needed as big a change as the Gentiles needed, and he baptized them in the Jordan to show it.

Now I agree that people like them needed such a change; but I am a Pharisee. I've always made it my business to keep God's law as carefully as I possibly could. Was Jesus suggesting that I also was in need of such repentance? It was disturbing to even consider it.

What, though, did he mean about being born of the Spirit? That had me even more puzzled, I can tell you. The prophets tell us that when Messiah comes the Spirit of God will move freely over the world, making prophets out of young men and women and giving visions and dreams. The Spirit will bring new life where everything has seemed like dry bones. The age of the Spirit would be the sign of Messiah's reign. It was certainly a great thing to hope for. John said that he baptized with water, but a greater one would baptize them with the Holy Spirit. I still could not see, though, how anyone can be *born* of the Spirit; so I asked him.

He was silent for a moment. "Can you hear anything?" he asked. As I listened I could pick out the sound of the wind blowing gently round the house, and branches of the trees rustling. He then said, "It's like that when anyone is born of the Spirit. You can hear the sound of the wind, but you don't know where the wind comes from, or where it goes. But you do know what effects it has. When the Spirit comes you know by the effects." I could understand a bit of what he meant, and the way he used our word 'ruach' to mean wind as well as Spirit. This, it seems, is what he meant by talking about being "born again." Now even for a theologian this was hard work.

"How can these things be?" I had to ask him.

He really appeared surprised by the question.

"You," he said, "who are the one who teaches Israel. Do you not understand these things?"

Well, I have been recognised for years as an eminent teacher. At the same time I confess I struggled to make sense of what he was saying. He was talking of an experience which was familiar to him but meant nothing to me. Heavenly matters he spoke of as if they were common-place to him. And if he was right, he was saying that if I did not experience this I would not see or enter the Kingdom of God. I had to try again to grasp his point. I tried again, as he explained further.

"I am telling you about earthly things, because your understanding is so earth-bound, so limited. I use examples and illustrations that you see every day, and still you can't make the connections. You don't see God at work there, in the world that you know so well. How, then, will you understand if I tell you about the world that I know well, but is totally foreign to you? You called me a Teacher come from God, and I am teaching you those very things. If I speak to you of heavenly things, how will you make sense of those, if you can't make sense of God's working in this world? And that is what I mean when I say that you need to be born again, and you need to be born of the Spirit. If you do not have that second birth into the realm of the Spirit, that world will remain foreign to you. That is the one entrance to understanding. Without it you really can't see God's Kingdom and you won't be capable of entering it."

He let the words sink in for a few moments, but I knew he had more to say. "Only someone who has come from that realm is able to speak of such things. You can't journey there to discover the truth; you depend on someone coming from there, the Son of Man."

It was beginning to make a bit of sense to me. I have never been to Rome or Athens, but I have met people who have been there. They can describe the cities to me – the architecture and the buildings, the customs of the people and so on. If a special person were sent from heaven, they could tell us what it was like. It still wouldn't tell me how to gain admission, but it would be a start.

"Do you remember a story from the Scriptures?" he asked me. At last, I was on familiar ground. The Scriptures could be my specialist subject on *Mastermind*! After all the puzzles, this was one thing I did know well. Surely I would not be lost on this.

"You remember how Moses lifted up the snake in the wilderness?" I nodded. It was a bad time in our history. Our ancestors had experienced that great redemption from Egypt, and God had led them through the desert. He had protected them and provided for them. Still they grumbled, and in their hearts wanted to return to bondage. So they were attacked by venomous snakes. Many died, and so they asked Moses to help. God told him to fashion a bronze image of the snake, and put it on a tall pole in the middle of the camp. Anyone who was bitten and looked at the bronze snake would be healed. Yes: I knew that story well enough. I wondered, though, what the connection might be.

"Just like Moses lifted up the serpent in the wilderness, the Son of Man will be lifted up. And whoever believes in him will have eternal life. That's how God loves the world. He has given his only Son, so that absolutely anyone who believes in him will no longer be condemned and perish. Instead, they will have eternal life." It sounds very much as if *believing* was the same as being *born again* or *born of the Spirit*. Those old Israelites who had been bitten *believed* what God had said, and *looked* at what he had provided, and were healed. Through Isaiah God had said, "*Look* to me and be saved, all the earth." Looking in the right place, at what God had provided and had backed with his promise, would bring salvation.

I needed to go away and think about all this. After all, who was this Son of Man? How was he going to be lifted up? Maybe time would tell.

It was a little while before I was involved with Jesus again. I kept hearing about the amazing things he was doing. From time to time I would make discreet enquiries about his teaching, and secretly I was impressed. Increasingly often his name cropped up in the Sanhedrin discussions.

One day they tried to arrest him. The chief priests were certain that he was a trouble-maker and he was leading the people astray. I was not so sure. I felt that if they gave him a fair hearing – as I had tried to do – they might see him as an ally, not an enemy. They made some contemptuous remarks about how ignorant the crowds must be, for paying attention to him. I knew it was sheer prejudice; so I asked, "Does our Law condemn a man without first giving him a hearing and learning what he does?" I realized that for the first time, in a small way, I had identified myself with Jesus. Their reaction was hostile, accusing me of being from the backwaters of Galilee: they knew better.

They did not manage to arrest him on that occasion, but got their chance at Passover. Late at night, they found him in Gethsemane, and brought him for a hurried trial. The Sanhedrin does not meet at night, so it was an illegal gathering. Maybe that is why nobody bothered to tell me about it until it was all over. If I had been there I would have made my protest. By all accounts it was a swift mockery of a trial, before they hurried him off to Pilate to have him crucified. And by the time I found out it was too late for me to do anything to help. I knew that Joseph was sympathetic, and we agreed to do this last kindness for a good man.

The cross was lowered to the ground. Lowered? If it was *lowered* it must first have been *lifted up* – the very expression he had used to me that first time we spoke. This might be the clue I had been searching for. During the hours he hung on the cross there had been an awful blackness over the land. Now it was clearing, and light was dawning in my soul too. A man had died, a Son of Man – a perfect representation of everything a man ought to be. He had been lifted up… "so that whoever believes in him shall have eternal life." They will share the life of God. They will have the life that belongs to God's Kingdom. To believe is to belong. It is to take God seriously. It is to engage with him in a true and personal relationship.

As we laid his body in the tomb, and these thoughts were rushing through my brain, I wished – Oh, how I wished – that somehow he might come back and tell me that at last I had got it right.

CHAPTER 15

Cleopas's Story

A week can be a long time, can't it? Waiting for a first date, or your wedding, how time drags. Waiting for exam results to come through, or for the doctor to tell you the outcome of the tests, it seems it will never happen. In other situations the time flies by: like a dentist's appointment coming up, or visitors arriving while you are still tidying the house.

And an unexpected visitor caught us unprepared in more ways than one. Let me tell you about it.

The wife and I were on our way home from Jerusalem, and it was a good walk; but we had plenty to talk about. Everything had been so overwhelming, so sudden. The twists and changes had taken everybody by surprise, and we were still trying to make sense of it. In fact, we were so focussed on this that I doubt we would have noticed if it had poured with rain. Certainly we had not been aware of the stranger who caught up with us and walked alongside us. I imagine he had been there, just yards from my shoulder, for some distance before he actually spoke. That was when we first noticed him.

"What are you two so engrossed in?" he asked. "You seem to be so occupied with your conversation that you don't notice anything else."

I stopped. I could hardly believe that anybody was unaware of all that had happened. Maybe my eyes were full of tears, or maybe it was the dust from the road; but I did not really pick out his features.

"Are you a stranger?" I asked, "Just visiting Jerusalem? Surely you must know what has happened."

I could scarcely credit that anybody was unaware. Everybody had been crowding to listen and to see Jesus this week. When he rode into the city last Sunday – was it really only a week ago? – it felt as if the whole city had turned out to meet him, to cheer and to shout Hosanna! All through the week he had been teaching in the Temple and again the crowds came to listen. How did this stranger manage to miss it?

"Why – what happened?" he asked.

I was going to have to tell him the story. Actually, I didn't mind telling it, because Jesus had meant so much to us. Telling the story might help us make a bit more sense of it, and it would certainly ease the pain a little.

"We have been talking about Jesus," I began. "He was like one of the prophets we have always been told about, and he was living here. He spoke such wise words, and everyone loved him. He did so many great things – healing the sick and curing the crippled. He could restore lepers and give blind people their sight back. He set people free who were trapped by evil spirits, and I even heard that he raised the dead. It was as if God had visited us once more, after such a long time. The power of God was at work in him. Like a lot of people, we hoped that this was the time when God was going to redeem Israel, and set us truly free at last." Even while I was talking I felt my old excitement coming back, just remembering those wonderful times. But sadness swept over me again.

We walked on in silence for a little while. I wondered how to tell the next part of the story. I felt he was encouraging me to tell it. So eventually I continued. "We were all so full of hope, half-expecting it to happen this week. But the whole situation changed so quickly. Our chief priests and leaders had him arrested. They tried him and condemned him and got Pilate to crucify him."

You know, I expected the stranger to be surprised, or even shocked, at this turn of events: it shocked us when it happened. The bottom had fallen out of our world, and we had no idea where to turn or how to pick up the pieces of our shattered dreams. Yet he seemed to take it all as, somehow, normal – the way he felt the story ought to have unfolded.

I wiped a tear from my eye, because I had more to tell him. "It only happened three days ago. The oddest bit of all is that this morning some of the women went to his grave, and his body had gone. They said that they had seen a vision. There were angels, telling them that he was alive. It amazed us, and it puzzled us. Now we know that he died; there is no doubt about that. So how could his grave be empty? Were the angels real, or just a vivid imagination?" My words just tailed off, because it wasn't making any sort of sense to me; so how must it sound to this stranger who knew nothing about any of the story. It was what the wife and I had been talking about when he joined us.

"Oh, you are so slow," he said gently, but firmly. "Wasn't it told long ago in the Scriptures that the Christ would suffer exactly like that, and so enter into his glory? Did you not believe what the prophets told you? It should not have taken you by surprise – and it was a triumph, not a failure."

Truth to tell, we were too upset to have remembered any of that. Every hope we had was that Jesus was the Messiah, who was going to set Israel free, and bring God's kingdom. It was all going to be so wonderful, so glorious.

Then he began to tell us from the Scriptures the way it all fitted into a pattern. It didn't matter whether it was Moses, or the Psalms, or the prophets: they all pointed to a Messiah who suffered and died for the sins of the people. They all told, or hinted, that his reign continued beyond death, that he must return to life again. We walked on, so captivated by the way he opened up the Scriptures to us that it was a surprise to find ourselves at the outskirts of Emmaus. We were nearly home, and we wanted to hear more and more of what the stranger had to say. There was a curious warmth, an excited burning in my heart as he talked to us. We reached the turning for our home. It looked as if he was going to continue his journey.

"Come in with us," my wife said. "It's getting late in the day. You shouldn't be journeying on, and we want you to come, have a meal with us. You can stay the night, and tell us more." I was glad she said it; but I felt the same. He came with us. I lit the little oil lamp, while my wife put the kettle on.

The flickering light played over his features, which seemed vaguely familiar. It did not take long to rustle up some bread, while the tea brewed. It was simple, basic fare, but there wasn't much else. And it was about to prove more than enough.

We sat down, and were about to give thanks to God for the simple gifts of life. That was when he picked up the bread, and he gave thanks to God. In that moment it all flashed through my mind, I was by the lakeside, as Jesus gave thanks and broke bread for thousands. I was in the Upper Room, as he broke the bread and told them it stood for his body, given sacrificially for them and for all. I was stood at Calvary, as they drove the nails through his hands. And now I noticed the nail-print in the hands that held and broke my wife's bread. Even as the recognition took my breath away, he vanished from sight. We looked at each other in sheer astonishment. We hardly needed to say it: we both knew who it was.

All that time we had been talking about him, he had been walking alongside us. While we were puzzling over whether he was alive, he was interpreting the story to us. And he had taken our bread, in our home, to tell us that he was alive.

No question what we had to do next. If we hurried, we could make those seven miles or so back to Jerusalem before it was dark. We just had to tell them that he was alive, and that we had known him as he broke bread with us.

I sometimes wonder, when we break bread in our services, if we shall see him that way again. And every time we eat bread at home, I picture him sat there with us; and he is with us, even if we no longer see him.

CHAPTER 16
The Rich Young Ruler

I met an old man recently. Several things struck me about him immediately. He stood upright, as though he had kept himself fit and healthy, and was neither over-weight through indulgence nor under-weight through neglect. There was an air of authority about him, suggestive of one who was accustomed to taking a lead and being in control. The smart cut of his clothes indicated that he had prospered in business. First impressions count for a lot, and there seemed warmth in his smile.

A second look, now that I had noticed his face, hinted that there was another strand to him. The warmth of his smile was not matched by his eyes, which were filled with sadness and disappointment, and lines of pain and regret etched across his face robbed it of real serenity. This was a man who may have prospered in business and been blessed with good health, but at the same time had not found real satisfaction in his life. Didn't the Scriptures say that, "It is the Lord your God who gives you power to get wealth"; so – if he had known God's blessing – why was he not content? I was curious to know his story. How much had I guessed correctly?

A little hesitantly, he began to tell me how he grown up in a loving, caring home. His parents had been devout and God-fearing folk. They had brought him up well: he had no complaints about them, or their example, or the encouragement they had given him to follow that way of life too. His father owned his own business, and he had inherited it, which is where he had found wealth and a position of authority and responsibility. He had mixed with the wealthy business men as an equal, without ever letting his standards slide. There was nothing underhand in his dealings, and he was regarded as a model employer. By hard work and honesty he had prospered further.

Not only did he treat his weekly attendance at worship as of pressing importance, he also took good care to study the Scriptures and to say his prayers privately. In every way he knew, he had tried to live by the things he read in the

Scriptures. Such integrity is rare. I was growing to like this man, and to admire his attempts to live a God-fearing life amid the pressures and temptations of life.

So, I asked him, if you had this cushion of security in your wealth, your possessions, and your comfortable life-style; didn't these satisfy you? No, he said, these things can't satisfy, because they do not touch the hunger in your soul. They never answer the big questions about where life is going, or how I can feel right with God, or what will happen when I die. I knew the lives of others who had wealth and possessions, and none of them seemed really content with what they had. Hoarding it turned you into a miser; and squandering it in self-indulgence only left a craving for more. There had to be more to life than that.

But surely, I replied, you lived an honest and upright life. You told me how careful you were to read the Scriptures, to pray and to worship. Anyone would say that you were a law-abiding man, who had tried his hardest to do what was right before God. How was it that you still had no peace?

Slightly reluctantly he agreed that, to all outward appearances he had lived a good and upright life, and it wasn't a hypocritical cover. As best he knew, he had always done what was right. And, yes, he had tried to honour God as much as he knew how. I sensed that he was willing to tell me a bit more. He continued: I had seen that the pursuit of pleasures didn't satisfy my acquaintances, and that wealth and possessions had not filled the emptiness inside me. I had to be honest with myself, and admit that all the time I had been saying my prayers and worshipping and reading the Scriptures I still had no sense that I would see God's Kingdom or share in that eternal life. Somewhere in my search I had missed the key.

I asked him: Have you ever met anyone who suggested to you that it might be possible to have that sort of contentment, that inner peace? Have you ever known anybody who seemed to enjoy the peace you were searching for? He winced. I had obviously touched a raw nerve. After a very long pause he began to tell me the whole story.

84

I had felt this disturbing feeling for some time. I had searched. I had asked questions. I found no answers. I came across Jesus. At the time I had heard about him, but never met him. It was Jesus who had posed the question to which I still had no answer: what shall it profit a man to gain the whole world, yet forfeit his soul? When he came into our town, he was teaching in the market place, as he so often did. A crowd soon gathered, and I joined them – discreetly, at the edge. I was immediately struck by his serenity, by his sincerity, and by his sheer confidence in God. As he spoke about God's coming Kingdom it seemed he was so familiar with it he might have been living there.

Did he have the secret of peace I wondered? I had to ask him; since nobody else had been able to help me. I must reach him, and see if he could explain it to me. He had finished teaching. They brought sick people to him, and as he laid his hands on the forehead of each, they were healed. At last he was finished, and he was about to journey on. Now, I thought; I've got to act now, or I shall regret it for ever. But what was I actually going to ask him?

"How can I be happy?" No: that was just too trite. "How can I feel contentment?" No again: it was still too obviously selfish. "How can I be part of God's Kingdom?" A bit better: but it still sounded too presumptuous. Then I got the flash of inspiration.

I ran up and fell at his feet. I looked up at him, and blurted out, "What must I do to inherit eternal life?" There: I'd said it. Now I would know! Eternal life: surely that was what the gnawing hunger in my soul was about. And to ask him what I had to *do* showed the humility I intended, that I wasn't so vain as to think I had it already.

I'm not sure, even now, what answer I thought he might give me. Perhaps he would tell me, like John the Baptist, that I should be baptized in the Jordan. I remembered the story of Naaman. He hadn't fancied a dip in that sluggish muddy river; but when he did, God not only healed him, but changed him too. Or were my good deeds, after all, good enough for God? Maybe Jesus would recognize my wealth, and tell me how to use it. Give generously. Perhaps I could endow a synagogue. Or would he welcome support for his movement? They looked as if they could do with a few shekels in the kitty, a wealthy patron on their headed notepaper.

"You know God's commandments? Keep them, and you will have life." Just like that, he said it.

Well, let me tell you... I'm as good as the next man when it comes to keeping the commandments. I've always been most careful about that, ever since I was a lad. No criminal record, no speeding on my donkey or parking my camel where I shouldn't. Murder? Out of the question. Adultery? I wouldn't even dream of it. Honour your father and mother? Pass that one with flying colours. No stealing, and you are definitely *never* going to read about scandals involving me in the paper. You know, I'm as good as the next man, and probably better than most of them. And I never miss the synagogue. And I say my prayers; and read the Scriptures. I like to think I'm pretty generous, too. The Law tells us to give ten percent, and I reckon I give nearer twenty. But wait a minute: if that is all there is to it, why am I still so dissatisfied?

That was when he dropped the bombshell. "Sell everything you possess, and give it all to the poor." I expect they heard my jaw drop up in Jerusalem. No; he can't be serious, can he? The look in his eye said he meant exactly that. Everything.

It flashed through my mind. I *need* my security. I might have inherited some of it, but I had worked hard to achieve what I had got. I had earned it, and it was mine. It had helped to give me my position in the community. I wasn't frivolous with my wealth, carelessly squandering it. I could give generously, and be hospitable. There was enough set by so that I should not be a burden on my relatives when I could no longer work.

And now I was forced to choose. I did wonder for a moment. After all, Jesus did not appear to have any riches, any possessions; and yet he looked so completely happy and at ease with himself. Was that really the secret I had been searching after for so long? But surely I could do good with my money? I'm not a miser, tight-fisted. I don't spend it all on myself. That's reasonable, isn't it, Jesus?

He stood there for quite some time, saying nothing, but searching me with those soft piercing eyes. There was tenderness, perhaps even a tear, as he watched me wrestling with my conscience. "It's easier for a camel to squeeze through the eye of a needle than for a rich man to enter the Kingdom of God," he said. He paused a moment, to see what I was going to do. I couldn't, I simply could not give it all away. Some of it, perhaps. A decent gift to some good cause – but it was so unfair to ask me to give all of it away.

And now, all these years later, I can't help thinking that he may have been right after all. I ought to have done it. I should have crucified my ambitions. Ironic, that, don't you think. It's me that should have crucified my ambitions, but he was the one who ended up crucified, the one who never did anything wrong.

Yes. I ought to have followed him. I'm certain he wanted to help me. He understood me far better than I recognized at the time. My money had taken God's place at the centre of my life. I was weak, not strong, because of my love for my possessions. Was It really impossible for me to abandon it all for the sake of God's kingdom? Not with God. 'There are no pockets in a shroud.' That's what they say, isn't it? I was at the funeral of one of my closest friends. We grew up together, committee members of the Jerusalem Chamber of Commerce. How much did he leave? I was curious to know, since he was a shrewd businessman. 'Everything,' came the reply.

And to think that we had once had the opportunity to come, like children, and follow Jesus.

You will have to supply your own ending to the story. The Bible has been a mirror for us. It's no longer the story of that sad old man. It has become your story, now, and mine. And only you can decide how it will end for you.

Where to find the original story

While Shepherds Watched....
> Based on Luke 2:1-20
> The reference to sheep at Bethlehem being kept for Temple sacrifices is from Alfred Edersheim's *The Life and Times of Jesus the Messiah*

A Wise Man Remembers
> Based on Matthew 2:1-12 and referencing Micah 5:2

An Inquisitive Neighbour
> Based much more fancifully on Matthew 2:1-12, but also using Luke 2 and Matthew 1:21

One Morning at the Lakeside
> Based on Luke 5:1-11; John 1:29, 40-42; Mark 1:21-28

Let Down by my Friends – Thank God!
> Based on Mark 2:1-12, but also bringing in Mark 1:32-34 and Isaiah 35:6

A Sinful Woman Forgiven
> Based on Luke 7:36-50, and noting Matthew 11:19 and Psalm 32:1

The Raising of the Widow's Son at Nain
> Based on Luke 7:11-17 and also Psalm 126:6; 1st Kings 19:17-34 and Deuteronomy 24:19-22

The Widow's Son at Nain
> The same story from another angle

The Woman at the Synagogue
> Based on Luke 13:10-17, with references to Psalm 121:1; 8:4; 16:3 and Isaiah 35:5-6

A Shepherd's Tale
> Based on Luke 15:1-7, and also drawing heavily on Psalm 23, John 10 and Isaiah 53:6, with a hint of Isaiah 40:11.

The meaning of 'Hephzibah' will be found in footnotes to
Isaiah 62:4

A Farmer's Widow
Based on Luke 12:13-21

The Tax-Collector and the Pharisee
Based on Luke 18:9-14, with references to Psalms 40:8;
15:1-5; 51:1-2, 10. The ritual for the Day of Atonement
is found in Leviticus 16, and I have also used Psalm
103:12

A Disturbed Night
Based on Luke 11:5-13; Psalm 121:4 and Matthew 7:7-
11

Nicodemus Reflects
Based on John 3:1-16; 7:50-52; 19:38-42; Matthew 3:1-
12 and Joel 2:28-29. Reference is made by Jesus to
Numbers 21:4-9 and Isaiah 45:22

Cleopas's Story
The account is in Luke 24:13-35

The Rich Young Ruler
Accounts are found in Matthew 19:16-30, Mark 10:17-31
and Luke 18:18-30. There is a reference to Deuteronomy
8:18 and Mark 8:36 and the story of Naaman in 2 Kings
5:1-14